Know Your Law

G000154664

Know Your Law

Greville Janner

Business Books

London Melbourne Sydney Auckland Johannesburg

Business Books Ltd

An imprint of the Hutchinson Publishing Group

17-21 Conway Street, London W1P 6JD

Hutchinson Group (Australia) Pty Ltd
30-32 Cremorne Street, Richmond South, Victoria 3121
PO Box 151, Broadway, New South Wales 2007

Hutchinson Group (NZ) Ltd
32-34 View Road, PO Box 40-086, Glenfield, Auckland 10

Hutchinson Group (SA) (Pty) Ltd
PO Box 337, Bergvlei 2012, South Africa

First published 1984
© Greville Janner

Set in Megaron

Printed in Great Britain by The Anchor Press Ltd
and bound by Wm Brendon & Son Ltd
both of Tiptree, Essex

British Library Cataloguing in Publication Data
Janner, Greville
Know your law
1. Corporation law – Great Britain
I. Title
344.106′66   KD2079
ISBN 0 09 151810 5 (Cased)
0 09 151811 3 (Pbk)

Building Your Business

Series Editor: Tom Cannon

The last decade has witnessed a growing awareness of the importance of a healthy small business sector. The individuality, flexibility and creativity of the entrepreneur are recognized as vital to economic prosperity. Yet the same period has thrown up more and more challenges to the small firm. Competition has become more rigorous, while the need for efficiency and the effective application of resources has increased sharply. Perhaps the most valuable of these resources today is knowledge.

This series of books has been designed specifically for the entrepreneur, to bring to the owner and manager of the small firm vital areas of knowledge and information. The aim throughout has been to break down the barriers between theory and practice. The books are 'action-oriented' and this action-orientation is built into the texts themselves. Each book is broken down into self-contained Units. Each Unit sets out **Key Issues**, develops the issues and ends with **Action Guidelines**. Wherever possible, examples are drawn from the actual experience of small business people. Each author is an expert in his own field but equally at home with the application of his expertise to the small firm.

Growing recognition of the needs of the small firm has led to a range of initiatives to provide assistance. Government at a national and local level, large companies, banks and voluntary agencies are actively seeking ways to help the owner and manager of the small business to thrive. However the key characteristic of this type of company is its dependence on individual effort and skill. The onus for survival and prosperity lies on the man or woman who turns these ideas into action. This series focuses on the key areas of customers, money, people and the law. The ideas presented will help provide the management expertise which leads to success.

For
Martin and Prissie Savitt
with admiration and affection

Contents

8

13

Preface

The small businessman who knows his basic law can save himself time, anxiety and money. Conversely, ignorance of the law is a recipe for unnecessary expense, aggravation and, potentially, worse.

This book is designed, then, to introduce those who own or manage small businesses to essential, practical law. It is intended both for reading and for reference. And it is carefully divided into those areas in which legal knowledge is vital, to avoid expensive trouble.

You cannot operate without premises – so should you buy a freehold or take on a lease? If you are a tenant, what are your rights when your term expires? Are you entitled to a new tenancy, and if so, then at what rent? What are your duties as an occupier to your visitors – whether they are customers, clients, the general public – or contractors or sub-contractors? And how should you deal with trespassers?

Your business may be small, but you will still need staff. How can you appoint and recruit, keeping within the law? What is a contract of employment and what essentials must be put into writing – and how?

What are the rules on dismissal – actual and 'constructive'? When is a dismissal 'wrongful' or 'unfair' – and what are the consequences of each and how do you avoid them?

Even the smallest business must sell to live. So what are the rules on contracts of sale and when is a deal binding – on you or on the other party? What are the laws on trade descriptions, representations and 'commercial puffs'? What is 'product liability' and how is the law likely to change?

However small your business, you must keep people safe. So what is the civil and the criminal law on health and safety at work? What

15

are your duties and liabilities under those statutes that apply to your particular type of business – whether it is (for instance) a shop, an office or a factory?

Unfortunately, every business must cope with crime at work. So here are the rules on theft – and on borrowing and finding, on corruption – and the business gift, on search, arrest and prosecution, and on 'receiving' and other crimes.

Finally (and here the book starts) you must know the best legal ways to set up and to run a business – and, if necessary, to put it into liquidation. What are the advantages and disadvantages of companies – or of partnerships or of operating as a self-employed person? What are the basic rules on taxation and on business expenses? And if the worst comes to the worst – how do you wind up your own business – or someone else's?

In a book of this size, of course, there is no room for anything academic. I have concentrated entirely on practical, everyday problems which you are bound to meet. I hope that with the help of this book, those meetings will be painless and inexpensive.

My thanks to HH Judge Brian Clapham, to my partner, Paul Secher, LLB, and to my son, Daniel Janner, MA(Cantab), barrister, for their help in preparing this book. And now, to you – good luck with the law. Even with the knowledge in this book at your side, you will still need good fortune if you are to earn it. Without the knowledge though, your chances of painless success are greatly diminished.

July 1983   GREVILLE JANNER

Section I

Your Business Structure

1
Companies, Partnerships and Individual Traders

- There are three possible legal frameworks for the small business: individual operation, partnership, or limited liability company.
- Which is the one most suited to your needs?
- What are the advantages and disadvantages of each?

Sole trader

Many businesses are started by one person. His contracts – like his profits and his debts – are his own. He enjoys the freedom of not having to consult, but bears the full burden of responsibility – to suppliers, customers and taxman alike. There is no limit on his personal liability to the creditors of the business, nor can he share it.

Limited liability company

The *Companies Act 1980* introduced new rules for the classification of companies. A 'public company', whose name must end with the words 'Public Limited Company' (or the abbreviation 'Plc') is a company limited by shares or guarantee and having a share capital, the memorandum of which states that it is to be a public company, and which has been registered as such. It must have a minimum issued share capital of £50,000. All companies that are not public companies are 'private companies'. The minimum number of members of both 'Plcs' and private companies is two.

Partnership

A partnership allows a man and his wife (or two or more* friends or colleagues) to operate a business in common with a view to profit. Even without any formal agreement, this arrangement is normally recognized by the law as a partnership. Whatever the division of time, skill or cash provided, the partners are free to run the business as they wish, within limits laid down by the Partnership Act.

Few people marry with a view to potential divorce; but every partnership should be entered into with an eye on dissolution. Proper arrangements should be made to meet possible disputes or disruption. While it is lawful to create a partnership without a formal agreement, it is generally most unwise to do so.

Before forming a partnership, consult a solicitor. Instruct him to draw up a partnership deed. By all means ask him for an estimate of the cost (which should be small). But a carefully conceived deed may be worth or may save a fortune.

If you are already in a partnership business without a written agreement, you may still formalize your arrangement. But *in the absence of agreement* to the contrary, the Partnership Act makes certain assumptions about your presumed intentions. These include, that:

- The profits are to be shared equally. No matter how much capital was put in by any particular partner or who does the work, profits are shared, pound for pound. So are losses – no matter whose errors or misjudgement may have caused them.

- The partners have equal right to use the business capital – not only the cash but all other assets. But when the business is dissolved, the partners will share the assets in proportion to their contribution to the capital.

- Each partner may make business contracts on behalf of the business – and all other partners will become liable to pay the creditors. You will not have to pay the *personal* bills of your partner – but be careful; there are many borderline cases, which hover between the personal and the business.

---

*Except for solicitors, accountants and bankers, there is an upper limit of 20 partners – but, of course, none for shareholders.

Advantages and disadvantages of each legal framework

Partnerships carry no limit on the liability of the individual partner for the firm's debts. If a partnership becomes insolvent, the creditors may take hold of the personal assets of each member of the firm. And that, of course, is the main disadvantage of a partnership operation.

On the other hand, there are many tax advantages through operating as a sole trader or in a firm. No Corporation Tax, less rigid control on expenses – both are likely to leave the trader or the partner with more in his pocket at the end of a successful day.

Still, as a company is a separate 'legal entity' from the people who run it, neither the directors nor the shareholders may generally be held liable for the company's debts. The director may be liable if his 'misfeasance' (generally, his fault) has caused the debt. And a shareholder may have to pay the amount (if any) still owing on his shares. But otherwise, the creditors lend (or give credit) to companies at their own risk.

While no formalities are required for a partnership, even a company is relatively easy to form. You may buy one 'off-the-shelf' or (and this is certainly preferable if your operation is to be of any size), you may have it formed for you by your solicitor or your accountant.

Companies must also (in general) file their accounts and so make their profits or losses visible to their creditors or their competitors. You may keep your personal business affairs or those of your firm to yourself. But if they are also the affairs of your shareholders, or you want the benefit of limited liability, then others may have to know how the business is doing.

The *Companies Act 1981* introduced certain exemptions from disclosure in accounts filed by small and medium-sized private companies. For this purpose, a small company is one with a turnover that does not exceed £1.4 million, with a balance sheet of not more than £700,000, and with not more than 50 employees. It may file accounts in abbreviated form and no profit and loss account is required.

Consulting your lawyer

Before asking any expert to help you to decide on the form of your business, make sure he is in full possession of all the facts. These include:

* Your general tax and financial position.
* The likelihood of your needing to rely upon any limits to your liability. Whether the creation of shares in the company will make it easier for you to raise the capital you will need or to divide up the proceeds.
* All other circumstances which should go into the legal and financial balance, before you make what will inevitably be one of your main business decisions.

2

Directors and the Law

• **What special legal rules apply to directors?**

A director is a person who directs the operations of a company. He is on the Board of Directors. He may or may not be a full-time director. Except in very rare cases (where there is a partnership and no salary and the relationship of employer and employee does not exist between the company and himself) he is *employed*.

Because a company is a *separate legal entity*, a director still is normally employed by *his* company, even if he owns all the shares. He has a *contract of employment* and his rights and those of the company depend primarily upon that agreement.

Where the business is small, directors often do not bother to make any formal arrangement. That is a mistake which becomes particularly obvious in times of dispute or if the company is merged or taken over.

A director's duties, liabilities and responsibilities are set out in great detail in the various Companies Acts. But remember:

- He must act honestly.
- He must not take secret profits out of the company's business.
- He must avoid fraud or 'misfeasance' or he may be prosecuted.
- He must ensure that the rules contained in the Companies Acts are complied with, including the holding of meetings and the keeping of proper accounts.
- And, while he normally has no personal liability for the company's debts, if he misbehaves then it may be possible for creditors to come down on him.

Wise directors use experienced solicitors and accountants to keep them out of trouble with the law.

3

The Advantages and Disadvantages of the Small Trader

- What are the legal advantages now enjoyed by the small trader, over his mammoth competitor?

- And what are the disadvantages?

- A man who is his own boss can, of course, eatablish a personal relationship with his clientele . . . decide on his opening hours with all the freedom allowed by the law . . . and regulate his own arrangements and those of his staff, for better or for worse.

- But how does the *small* business fare, under the law of the land?

The small trader may benefit from the law in two main respects: as an employer and as a sole proprietor or partner.

Help for the small trader

Believing that small employers would take on more staff and shed fewer if employees were less well protected, the Government introduced in 1980 a series of new measures, designed to help the small trader. They are:

- The qualifying period which an employee must serve so as to get unfair dismissal protection was doubled – in broad terms, from six to twelve months. But if an employee works for an employer who (alone or with any associated employer) at no time during his employment had more than 20 full-timers on his books, then that qualifying period is now two years. So the small trader, employing no more than 20 people, may now dismiss an employee for any reason or for none, fairly or unfairly, during his first 24 months of service (or, say, 23 months to be safe). Naturally, the employee is entitled to his notice or pay in lieu. But no tribunal can help if he is sacked unfairly.

- If a trader employs no more than five people, he can normally avoid taking back a woman who has been absent due to pregnancy or confinement and who wishes to exercise her right to return, even if she has followed all the required procedures, including serving the appropriate notices. If it is not reasonably practical for the employer of no more than five to give the mother her job back, he does not now have to to do so.

- Firms of the same small size – employing five or less – are also exempt from the rules on sex discrimination. If they are so ill advised, they may exclude women or married people. But note: there is no exclusion for *race* discrimination.

- Partnerships of less than six are also excluded from the rules on race discrimination – and may (unhappily) exclude partners on the grounds of race, nationality or ethnic or national origin.

Rights of employees

With the exceptions given above, employees of small traders have the same rights as anyone else. These include:

- The right to written particulars of their main terms of service, within 13 weeks of the start of the employment or 4 weeks of any change.

- The right to proper notice, i.e. the period agreed; in the absence of agreement, such period as is reasonable in all the circumstances; and in any event, no less than the statutory minimum, which is: 7 days after 4 weeks' service; 2 weeks after 2 years; and then add a week a year until 12 weeks after 12 years.
- Maternity pay and maternity leave.
- Minimum statutory redundancy rights – after two years' service after reaching the age of 18, rising to a maximum of £4,200 after 20 years' service (as from 1 February 1983), at the appropriate age and pay.
- Protection against unfair dismissal, including: (a) *compensatory* award – (£7,500 maximum); (b) *basic* award, for lost redundancy entitlement – £4,200 (as above); (c) *additional* award if the tribunal makes an order for the unfairly dismissed employee's re-engagement or reinstatement and the employer unreasonably fails to comply with it.
- Protection under the Health and Safety at Work Act against the hazards of his job – the trader (individually as well as as a company) being criminally liable if a hazard was caused as a result of his neglect or with his consent or connivance.
- Protection in civil law against accidents at work – even the smallest trader is required to carry insurance against employers' liability.

Disadvantages The main disadvantage of the small trader is generally his inability to cope with (for instance) an unfair dismissal award of a few thousand pounds, which would not unduly worry his larger competitor. Apart from taking special care, the small trader should consider insuring against the risks of unfair dismissal – which can be done quite cheaply.

Finally, the small trader seldom has to worry about the complications of trade union law and practice. He negotiates individually with his staff and avoids the problems of collective bargaining. But his employees are legally entitled, if they wish, to join trade unions. And in cases of dismissal for *discrimination*, the normal qualifying periods for unfair dismissal protection do not apply.

Advantages Employment law apart, the main legal advantages of the small trader lie in the flexibility of his organization. In particular, if he does not need the benefits of limited liability, he can operate as a sole trader or in partnership. In addition to the advantages of doing so, already discussed, there are others:

* PAYE is not deducted. The individual generally pays tax between 18 and 30 months after he has earned his money. Meanwhile, he has had its use for that period; and in times of inflation, the tax paid is, of course, worth much less than when the money was earned.
* As the money is his, expenses are more easily tax-deductible. The sole trader or partner may deduct expenses incurred *wholly and exclusively* in the performance of his duties; the employee must show that the expenses were incurred *wholly, exclusively and* **necessarily** in carrying out his job.

Remember, though, that if you operate through a company, it has a different legal existence from yourself – even if you own all the shares. And it will need a separate set of accounts from those which you submit on your own behalf.

The small trader may also employ his wife and family in the business. Indeed, if his relations work for him and he fails to pay them, he is quite unnecessarily giving away his money to the Revenue. If you employ your wife or other relative, then you should pay her or him exactly the same as you would pay anyone else who did the same job. And as that individual will have an entirely separate set of tax reliefs, you as a family will normally be much better off. Check up, though, with your accountant as to the amount that it would be both proper and worthwhile to pay your children.

As we saw earlier, as a small trader you have far more flexibility and independence than a larger concern. Shareholders in a company are only liable for the company's debts to the extent of any sum which they may owe for their shares. The sole trader or partner is liable for his debts or those of the firm to the extent of everything that he owns in the world.

The small business, then, controls its own destiny – for better or for worse. And the law is turning more in his direction. But his eggs, legal and commercial, are in a much smaller basket. So he also bears a far greater weight of his own responsibilities.

4

Names Matter

- The smaller the business, the more valuable its name is likely to be – as an actual or as a potential asset.
- How do you protect your own name and avoid trespassing on those of others?
- What are the main legal rules on name-calling?

Your name

You yourself may acquire a name in two ways. You may be given it by your parents or you may afterwards change it. The change may be automatic – by marriage or by (non-marital) choice. If you wish to alter your surname, you may do so without any formalities whatsoever. You may adopt any surname you choose. In legal proceedings, you will probably be called 'James Winter (formerly James Winterbottom)' – but Winter will be your name.

However, formalities are recommended. These avoid any subsequent doubts or disputes. The normal procedure is to get a solicitor to prepare a document called a 'deed poll' in which you state that you renounce your old name and adopt a new one.

Christian names cannot be changed by deed poll or otherwise. There is nothing to prevent you adopting any pseudonym that suits you. But technically, your 'Christian' or 'given' name is with you for life – once it is registered at birth it can only be changed at baptism. Hence parents should be very careful in the choice of the names they give to their offspring.

Business names

For different reasons, similar care should be taken when choosing a business name – whether for a company, firm or business. While in general you may choose any name that pleases you, there are specific and extremely important limits to your choice. The first arises 'at common law' – that is, apart from any statute.

Passing off

No one is entitled to *pass off* the goods or services he offers as those of another. Where the name is the same, or very similar, confusion may be caused – and the people who used or adopted the name after it had become attached to others will, in effect, be cashing in on the goodwill built up by those others. This the law forbids.

Means of deception

Passing off may take various forms. Briefly, it involves the adoption of a name that has become used by and connected with the business of another.

Your products or services may be made distinctive by their own 'get up' or that of your brochures, advertisements or other documents. Any doubt as to whether or not the name would be likely to confuse may be swiftly dispelled if the 'get up' of the marketing material bears similarities to that used for similar services provided by others in the trade with like names.

Is your name your own?

In general, you are fully entitled to use your own name as you see fit. It is part of yourself ... of your personality ... of your goodwill ... but this right is not absolute. You may be prevented from using that name, if the result would be to cause deception.

One judge put the rule like this: 'An injunction ought not to be granted to prevent a person from using his own name, unless there is evidence that the defendant was using the name for fraudulent purposes'.

In another case, it was held that 'no man has the right to represent his goods as the goods of another person; if he simply uses his own name, that is no prima facie evidence of intention to misrepresent his goods. But if besides using his own name he does other things which show that he is intending to represent, and is in point of fact making his goods represent the goods of another person, then he is to be prohibited – but not otherwise.'

In one hilarious case, a Mr Sidney Lyons changed his name to Joseph Lyons and started selling various foods, under what was now his own name: 'J. Lyons'. J. Lyons Ltd of Cadby Hall succeeded in satisfying the court that their namesake 'had intended to deceive and had deceived the public into buying his goods as and for the plaintiffs' goods'. An injunction was granted – together with damages and costs.

Adopted names

Now suppose that a businessman near to you sees fit to call his business by the name that you have built up over the years. 'We specialize and you do not', he retorts when you complain. 'You have a different clientele.'

'Where one trader complains of the use of a trade name by another trader carrying on a similar business,' said a Court, 'as being calculated to mislead and deceive the public, the objects of the two businesses need not be absolutely identical to entitle him to relief if there is great similarity'. If the other outfit is, in fact, passing off its business as yours, the courts will step in to help you.

Business names and company names

The *Companies Act 1981* made important changes in the rules affecting both business names and company names.

Business names Under the old system businesses had to register at the Registry of Business Names. The Registry was abolished by the 1981 Act, after much heated parliamentary debate – the measure was fiercely contested by consumer groups and individual MPs, who believed that the abolition would render it much harder for those dealing with businesses to discover the true identity of the owners. The Registry has been replaced by a self-regulating system. So:

- If you run your business using your own name, with or without Christian name or initials, you need not worry.
- But if your name forms only part of the business name, then you will have to comply with the 1981 Act's provisions (see below).
- Likewise with partnerships, if the business name comprises only the names of the partners, the partnership is not affected by the new rules.
- Companies are affected if they use a business name which is not the same as the corporate name of the company, e.g. if 'J.S. Ltd' uses the trading name 'J.S. Pictures', then it must comply with the new provisions.
- Another exception to the new disclosure rules is where the owner's name is only changed to the extent that he wishes to show that the business is being carried on in succession to a previous owner, e.g. 'A. Jackson (formerly W. Davies)'.

If your business name does not fall within one of the excepted categories, then you must comply with the new disclosure rules by disclosing the name of the owner(s) and the business or other address(es) within Great Britain.

The address(es) must be one(s) at which documents could be served. The names and addresses must be shown on all:

- Business letters.
- Written orders for the supply of goods and/or services.
- Invoices and receipts issued in the course of business.
- Written demands for payment of debts arising in the course of business.

You must also display the information prominently so that it can be read easily in any premises where the business is carried on, and to which customers or suppliers have access. The required names and addresses must also be given immediately in writing to anyone with whom anything is done or discussed in the course of the business, if that person asks for them. Where a partnership has more than 20 partners, the names of all the partners need not be placed on business documents, provided that the documents state the address of the principal place of business and that a full list of the partners' names and addresses may be inspected at that place of business.

Anyone who fails to comply with these disclosure provisions commits a criminal offence which may result in a fine of £200. A business that fails to display or to make available details of ownership may be unable to enforce its contracts. A contract will be unenforceable against another party to the contract who can show that he has been unable to pursue a claim against the business or has suffered financial loss as a result of the breach, unless the court is satisfied that it would be just and equitable to enforce the contract.

Company names Registration of a company name was, and remains, necessary; however, the procedure has been simplified by the 1981 Act which is intended to speed up registrations. It is no longer necessary, in most cases, for those forming companies to obtain the provisional approval of the Registrar to a particular name before the necessary legal documents are prepared.

The onus of checking on the suitability of a name is really transferred from the registrar to the applicant. The registrar publishes an index of names of companies and it is not permitted to register a company under a name already on the index. A new company may also be rejected by the Secretary of State for Trade if it suggests a connection with the Government or with a local authority or is offensive or contains certain words or expressions prohibited by regulations.

A special resolution of the company is required to effect a change of name. Under the 1981 Act, the Secretary of State may, within twelve months of the date of registration, direct a company to change its name on the grounds that it is identical to or too like that of a name appearing on the register.

Undesirable names

Whatever your sort of establishment, avoid 'Red Cross', and however splendid the name 'Royal' might sound when applied to your business, the odds are that you will not be allowed to use it unless, of course, you have royal patronage. Even 'Commonwealth', 'National' or 'International' are names that will not normally be permitted – nor will 'names which suggest a connection with a Government department or local authority' (perish the thought).

Deceptive names

If a company manages to get registered by a name the Department of Trade later decides is too like the name by which a company is already registered, the new outfit may be required to change its name. So if you find someone else coming into the field with a registered name which is too like your own, do not despair. Your solicitor may be able to induce the Department of Trade to take action.

Change of name

Any company may change its name by special resolution, provided that it obtains the written consent of the Department of Trade. Various formalities have to be complied with – for instance, the change is not complete until a new certificate of incorporation is issued. The change will not affect any of the rights or obligations of the company. Legal proceedings by or against it will be unaffected. Nor will the change prevent legal proceedings being brought or continued, if they have been effective against the company under its previous name. A corporation by any other name. . . .

Registration of trade marks

No trade mark may be registered unless it contains one or more of the essential particulars specified under the various Trade Marks Acts. One of these is: 'the name of a company, individual or firm, represented in a special or particular manner'.

Suppose that you operate simply under the name 'Brights'. The name as such would not be registerable – but if you invented some special script or style for the printing of the name, that might well constitute a registerable mark. This sort of peculiarity is called 'get up' by lawyers and is one of the more easily understood of technical legal phrases.

Nowadays, this sort of protection (whilst very useful for other kinds of marks) is not usually what matters with names. Passing off actions are far more useful.

If you do wish to register a trade mark, then you should obtain the required application forms from the Trade Marks Registry (part of the Patent Office), 25 Southampton Buildings, Chancery Lane, London WC2 (telephone: 01-405 8721). Before making an application, you would be well advised to make a search at the Registry to find out if the mark has already been registered.

5

Tax-deductible Travel

- **Why are the expenses of getting to work not tax-deductible?**

Business expenses

If you are self-employed, then you may deduct any expenses incurred *wholly and exclusively* for the purpose of your business. If you are an employed company director or other employee, however great or small, you may deduct those expenses incurred *wholly, exclusively* **and necessarily** in the performance of your duties. Either way, the only expenses that are deductible are those incurred while you are earning your living and not those paid out 'preliminary' to your work.

So that rules out not only the expenses of getting to and from work, but also the cost (for instance) of applying for jobs or undergoing training so that you are better qualified when you do apply. When you travel from office to works or from works to customer, from customer to supplier or from one place of business to another, then you are performing your duties or earning your living and the expenses are properly deductible. But if you are getting from your home to a place of work, then they will be deductible only if you can prove that your home is itself a 'nub' or 'nexus' of your activities.

Working at home

If you keep your files, your tools or your equipment at home ... if you have your records or your library there ... if you operate from your home as an office – and if you can satisfy the tax man that your use of your home for your work is genuine – then not only will you be entitled to deduct travel expenses to and from home to places of work, but a proportion of your home expenses will also be tax-deductible. If you think that you may come within that category, have a word with your own or with your company's accountant. And do not forget to discuss the effect of the business use on your freedom from liability to capital gains tax when you sell your home.

Section 2

Your Premises

6

Freehold v. Leasehold

- **Every business, however small, needs premises.**
- **So which is better, freehold or leasehold?**
- **And what is the difference between them?**

Freeholders

The best property right known to the law is that of a 'freeholder'. He holds the premises free from the rights of others. Exceptions:

- Your neighbours are entitled *not* to suffer as a result of 'nuisance', i.e. unreasonable disturbance through the use of your property. If, for instance, your neighbour objects to smells or noise or dust or vibrations, then – provided that the extent of the disturbance goes beyond that which a reasonable average person would expect to put up with as 'part of the give and take of neighbourly life' – a court will grant him an 'injunction' to restrain your unneighbourly behaviour. And proceedings may also be taken under the Public Health Acts.
- Even if you own the freehold, you will still have to comply with planning regulations (see page 54).

Leaseholders

If, on the other hand, you are the leaseholder, your rights depend upon the terms of your lease or tenancy agreement. You are a tenant and must comply with your agreement. This means not only that you must pay the appropriate rent, but also that you must obey the other covenants – especially those involving repairs.

Happily, you are protected by the *Landlord and Tenant Act 1954* (details on pages 44–53).

Many leases are even more valuable than some freeholds. But beware of repairing clauses; watch out for restrictions on your right to change the use of the premises or to assign or sub-let; and remember that a lease is a contract, the same as any other. Your rights depend primarily upon its terms.

7

Conveyancing

- **Whether you are buying or selling, letting or renting, you are in for trouble if you do not work out the legal angles in advance.**

- **So what are they?**

Buying and selling

First, be sure that you pay your deposit 'subject to contract'. If the deal goes off, whether through your fault or that of the other people, you will normally get your money back. Remember, too, that there is no 'standard deposit' of 10 per cent or any other percentage. Many vendors happily accept £100 deposit perhaps going up to 10 per cent when contracts are actually exchanged.

Next, take care what estate agents' form you sign. If you are a purchaser, you should only agree to pay an agent in the rarest of circumstances. If he is taking special steps to find you a business, then perhaps you might 'retain him'. Otherwise, leave it up to the seller to meet the agency fee.

Sole agency   If you are the seller, then never grant *sole selling rights*. Do that and you will have to pay the agent, even if you find the purchaser. Only rarely should you grant a *sole agency*, because if (while that agency subsists) you let another agent find the purchaser for you, you will have two lots of agency fees.

Grant a 'sole agency', for a limited period, only if the agent is really going to spend real money on selling your business or if he will reduce his fees. Even if you make someone your 'sole agent', you retain the right to sell the property yourself. If *you* find the purchaser, you are not liable for agency fees.

Mind, too, what oral agreements you make and especially what documents you sign. If, for instance, you agree to pay an agency fee the moment a deposit is taken, that is your downfall. Fees should only be recoverable by agents if and when the property is actually sold.

The *Estate Agents Act 1979* came fully into force in 1982. Under the Act, clients must be told in advance what an estate agent's charges for services will be and the circumstances in which they will fall due. Estate agents must also hold clients' deposits in clearly identified accounts and pay any interest that accumulates (if more than £10). The Director General of Fair Trading is able to ban any 'unfit' person from estate agency work.

Employing a solicitor   Whether you are buying or selling, *do employ a solicitor*. He will examine whether the area in which you are proposing to acquire a shop or office is to be developed or affected by a road widening scheme. He will check on the vendor's right to sell. And he will protect your position generally. Equally, if you are the seller, your solicitor will look after your interests and, in particular, do his best to tie up the purchaser, well and truly.

Renting

If you are renting your new premises, watch out especially for the repairing clauses. For instance, if you agree to 'maintain' the property in 'good and tenantable repair', then it will not be good enough to return your shop or offices at the end of the letting in the same condition as it was in when you acquired the place. You may have to put it into good order first. So get your solicitor to explain the repairing covenants so that you understand precisely what obligations you are undertaking.

Restriction of rights   Watch out, too, for any clause which restricts your right to assign. If you can only assign or sub-let with the land-lord's consent, then the law will imply a term into the arrangement that such consent 'shall not unreasonably be withheld'. But if there is an 'absolute prohibition against assignment', the landlord has got you just where he wants you – and may be as unreasonable as he likes.

Tenants' rights   Whether you are the landlord or a tenant, never forget the rights which a tenant acquires under the *Landlord and Tenant Act 1954*. Business tenants are difficult to drive from their shops, offices or other premises. And if a new rental cannot be agreed, the tenant has the right to apply to the court to fix appropriate terms.

There are many problems. For instance, it is up to you to specify what fixtures and fittings are covered by your agreement, so as to avoid any future dispute. And ask your solicitor to arrange that the whole transaction is put into the best possible form, from your tax angle. You may make a quite unnecessary free gift to the Revenue simply by arranging to buy or sell without having the rules on stamp duty (for example) well in mind.

Calling in a surveyor   Finally, do remember to call in a surveyor. You may be the world's greatest expert in your area of business, but it would be very surprising if you could spot incipient rot (wet or dry) or apparently minor subsidence. There is no law against selling a tumbledown house. Only when you buy premises in the course of construction is the law likely to help you – and then only if you do not sign away your rights. To acquire premises and then to discover afterwards that they are defective is a misery which your lawyer can do little to mitigate.

From the legal angle, then, there is a lot more to assignment of a business than most vendors and purchasers ever realize – until too late. Still, you have appreciated the most vital rule of all. Go to your lawyer and let him deal with your conveyancing. There is much truth in the old saying:

❛ The man who is his own lawyer has a fool for a client'. ❜

8

Selecting Solicitors

- **If you move from one area to another, do you need separate solicitors to do the conveyance in each?**

- **How much will it cost you to employ solicitors to do the conveyance of your premises?**

- **And how can you find out that cost in advance?**

There is no reason in law or practice why solicitors should not act for you in the transfer of property in a different town. They can, if necessary, employ local agents to do the necessary footwork. So if you have confidence in your solicitors, why not let them get on with both jobs?

Alternatively, if you do not have a completely happy relationship with a firm, then you could try to get a recommendation from business people where you are going. These solicitors could then do both jobs.

How much will they charge?

It is impossible to assess conveyancing charges without knowing such factors as the price of the property you are purchasing, the complications of the work involved, whether you are also selling your own old premises before buying your new ones and the experience and level of charges of the solicitors themselves.

So you should go to the solicitors of your choice; give them full details of the transactions; and ask them what they would charge you. If you wish, you can then shop around and see whether you get a more reasonable quote from other lawyers.

9

Sub-letting

- If you are a tenant without any formal tenancy agreement, are you entitled to sub-let?

- If you rent your premises and you find you cannot afford the rent increase demanded when your rent is reviewed, how should you present your case?

- And where can you appeal if you lose?

Tenancy agreements

If you are a *tenant*, you have a *tenancy agreement*, whether or not you have anything in writing. If nothing was said to you about sub-letting when you took on the tenancy, you may sub-let without your landlord's consent. But, equally, as your sub-tenant will acquire the same rights under the *Landlord and Tenant Act 1954* (as amended) as those which it gives you against your landlord, you should certainly get your lawyer to draw up an agreement with your sub-tenant, for your protection as well as his.

You will probably want to include in your sub-tenant's agreement an absolute prohibition against assignment or sub-letting. If he is forbidden to give up possession of all or part of the property, then he cannot do so and if he asks for permission at some future date you may refuse it, as reasonably or unreasonably as you may wish. If the agreement says that he shall not sub-let without your permission, then the law implies another term into the agreement – that your permission may not be 'unreasonably withheld'.

A sub-letting in breach of a covenant is a breach which in law cannot be remedied and which may therefore result in forfeiture of the lease. When a lease is forfeited, any underlease created out of it automatically comes to an end. But the underlessee has the common law right to apply for relief against forfeiture. Relief may be granted if the court decides that it would be just and equitable to do so.

Rent review

Your rights against your landlord will depend upon the terms of your lease. Normally, if the parties to a lease cannot agree on the appropriate rental when it comes up for review, the lease will say how the dispute will be resolved. For instance, if the parties cannot agree upon an independent arbitrator, then one may normally be appointed by a person holding a stated office.

10

At Your Lease's End

- **If your lease comes to an end, are you entitled to a new one – and if so, then on what terms?**
- **The answers are mainly in the** *Landlord and Tenant Act 1954* **(as amended).**

The 1954 Act applies 'to any tenancy where the property comprised in the tenancy is or includes premises which are occupied by the tenant, and are so occupied for the purposes of a business carried on by him or for those and other purposes'. Provided that you yourself occupy and carry on a business in the premises, then, even if you live there as well, the Act is designed for you.

Giving notice

A business tenancy no longer comes to an end, unless either the landlord or the tenant takes some specified step that terminates it. The landlord may do so by serving notice on the tenant not less than six, nor more than twelve months, before the date when the tenancy would otherwise expire, specifying the date at which it is now to come to an end.

This notice must require the tenant, within two months of its being received, to tell the landlord in writing whether he will be willing to give up possession. It must also state whether or not the landlord would oppose an application to the court on the part of the tenant for a new tenancy, and if so, on which of the specified grounds.

If you are a tenant and the landlord has not served such a notice on you and you wish to remain in the property, then say nothing and do nothing. Of course, you will not have any absolute certainty or security. If you want that, then you yourself must give notice to the landlord, requesting a new tenancy. Within two months of your request, he is entitled to give notice to you that he would oppose an application to the Court for the grant of a new tenancy. Once again, this notice must state which of the grounds specified by the Act he intends to rely upon.

There are seven specific grounds for obtaining possession. These are:

- That the tenant has not kept the property in good repair.
- That the tenant has been persistently late in paying his rent.
- That there have been 'other substantial breaches' by the tenant 'of his obligations under the current tenancy'.
- That the landlord is willing to provide suitable alternative accommodation.
- That the landlord wishes to let off the property as a whole, and the tenant's current tenancy was created by sub-letting only part of it.
- That, on the termination of the current tenancy, the landlord intends to demolish or reconstruct the premises. (Note that a landlord cannot now resist a tenant's application for a new business tenancy on this ground if the tenant is prepared to accept a new tenancy of all or part of the premises, and the landlord can do the work 'without interfering to a substantial extent or for a substantial time' with the tenant's business. The tenant must agree to the new tenancy containing a term which would give the landlord reasonable 'access and other facilities for carrying out the work intended'.)
- That the landlord, not having acquired his interest in the property less than five years ago, intends to occupy the premises himself.

Suppose the landlord fails to prove his contention and a new lease has to be granted. The next questions are what will be its terms, what rent will the tenant have to pay and how long will it be for?

A new lease

In most cases, landlord and tenant bargain, either in person or through their solicitors. The terms of the new tenancy are hammered out between them. But if no agreement can be reached, the Act provides that the Court shall decide all points.

The tenancy shall be such as is 'reasonable in all the circumstances', but for a maximum of 14 years. The rent generally speaking is 'that at which . . . the holding might reasonably be expected to be let in the open market by a willing lessor'.

Length of lease

Next, what term will the tenant get? He will usually seek the longest possible term and will try for the 14 years maximum. He will tell the Court how long he has been there, how he has built the place up, how his need is a great one whereas the landlord will lose little by the grant of a long term – and so on. The judge must consider all the circumstances and decide what is reasonable.

If a new lease is not granted

Suppose now that the tenant can get no new lease and has to leave the premises. What compensation can he claim for his lost goodwill?

First, the tenant must prove that the only reason that he has not got a new tenancy is because the Court is precluded from granting him one through the landlord bringing himself within one of the last three exceptions. In other words, if he cannot get a new lease and this is entirely in order to suit the landlord's convenience and not through any default on his own part, then he is entitled to compensation.

Compensation The extent of the compensation depends on how long the tenant has been in business in the premises. Roughly speaking, if he or some predecessor in his business has been in occupation for 14 years or more, then he will be entitled to twice the rateable value multiplied by $2\frac{1}{4}$. If he has been there for less than this time, the compensation is $2\frac{1}{4}$ times the rateable value of the holding.

Making improvements   If an improvement has been carried out by the tenant, he cannot be afterwards forced to pay a higher rent because he has seen fit to spend money on his premises. Exception? If the work was done to comply with a covenant in the lease.

The surest and most popular way to lose your rights is to delay when you receive notice under the 1954 Act. If you have missed your chance, you will never get it back. There is no prospect of getting leave from the Court to serve your notice late. If you are late, you are finished. But if you have the good sense to put the matter in the hands of your lawyer in good time, the Act can bring you enormous benefits. The end of your lease need not bring disaster after all.

Short tenancy   From the above it is clear that a landlord has a powerful incentive to avoid the effects of the landlord and tenant legislation. He may try to do so in several ways – by creating a short tenancy; or by attempting to create a licence as opposed to a tenancy; or by insisting that the prospective tenant avails himself of the limited statutory provisions for contracting out of the protection given by the 1954 Act. Those may apply where the landlord and tenant jointly apply to the court, which may authorize the parties to enter into an agreement excluding the provisions of the Act regarding the continuation and renewal of the tenancy agreement. If you are invited to 'contract out of the 1954 Act' make sure you seek the advice of your solicitor before acting.

Asking your solicitor

So look at your lease or tenancy agreement and see where it leads you. But if you cannot work out the answer from the terms of your agreement with your landlord, then you should take that agreement to your solicitor and let him advise you in a way that is only possible for a lawyer in full possession of all the facts.

Renting from a local authority

If you rent your business premises from a local authority the disadvantage is that you do not have the same *security of tenure* as other business tenants. If the tenancy of business premises rented from a private owner comes to an end, then the tenant is well protected by the *Landlord and Tenant Act 1954* (as amended). His landlord may only get possession on stated grounds and, if necessary, by getting an order for possession from a court.

However: Section 57 of the 1954 Act deals with 'modification' of these rules 'on grounds of public interest'. In particular, where the property 'belongs to or is held for the purposes of a government department or is held by a local authority, statutory undertaking or a development corporation', then 'the Minister or Board in charge of any government department may certify that it is requisite for the purposes of the . . . department . . . or authority' that the occupation shall be changed.

That means in practice that a certificate may easily be obtained from the Department of the Environment. If a certificate is granted, the tenant cannot renew the lease, and obtaining a certificate under Section 57 is usually a far quicker process than the court proceedings.

II

Premises and Planning Permission

- When do you need planning permission?

- What, for instance, if you wish to convert a warehouse into a shop or office?

- Are you entitled to use your home for a mail order or other business?

Changing the use of premises

When you materially change the use of premises, then you create a *development*. When you *develop* land, you need planning permission. You *develop* when (for example) you change the use of property from (say) retailing to manufacturing – or from storage or warehousing to residential or retailing.

Getting planning permission

A material change of use will require planning permission, except for instance where both uses fall within the same *use class*. For example, most shops fall into the same *use class*. But a change from one kind of shop to another may, although rarely, constitute a change requiring planning permission. The shops class does *not* include (among others) shops for the sale of hot food, pet animals and birds, motor vehicles or tripe!

So before you buy, make sure that you will get the permission you need. Otherwise you may find yourself left with an old warehouse and without the consent you need to turn it into shops. A preliminary discussion with the appropriate planning officer at your local district council offices could be invaluable.

Rented home premises

If your home is rented, then there may be restrictions against business use contained in your lease. So if your landlords found out that you were using your premises in breach of covenant, they might make trouble for you. But if you own your own premises – if you are the *freeholder* – then at least this worry would not apply.

If you use residential premises for business purposes, that is a *change of use* and you are *developing* the property. Planning permission is required for a development.

Once again, if it is discovered that you are using premises in breach of planning requirements, notice could be served on you to put an end to this improper behaviour. If you do not comply with an enforcement notice, you may be prosecuted and liable to a penalty which will increase each day the violation continues.

12

Developments and Planning Consent

- **What are the main rules on planning that the small business needs to know?**

Consent for development

'Planning permission is required for the carrying out of any development of land', says the *Town and Country Planning Act 1971*. There are exceptions (as we shall see). But the rule to remember is: to *develop* you need consent.

'Development' defined

In general, *development* means 'the carrying out of building, engineering, mining or other operations in, on, over or under land, or the making of any material change in the use of any buildings or other land'. So the definition can be divided conveniently into two parts: (1) works of building and the like and (2) changes of use.

The exception to the rule

'The carrying out of works for the maintenance, improvement or other alteration of any building, being works which affect only the interior of the building or which do not materially affect the external appearance of the building . . .' are not regarded as *development*.

So you will not need planning permission to alter the position of internal walls, to instal central heating, or even to tart up the exterior of your premises, provided that the appearance is not 'materially affected'. Exception: if your premises are *listed* as of special interest, are in a Conservation Area, or occupy a *scheduled building* – in which case you will need permission to alter the outside of the premises. Permission is always required for any illuminated sign or advertisement.

Advertisements

'The use for the display of advertisement of any external part of the building which is not normally used for that purpose' is treated as 'involving a material change in the use of that part of the building'. So before you erect new signs or plaster the side of your building with advertisements, check with your local planning authority.

Rules for homes

'For the avoidance of doubt it is hereby declared' that when you convert a dwelling house which has been used as one unit into two or more units, there *is* a 'material change' in the use of the building. But 'the use of any building or other land within the curtilage of a dwelling house for any purpose incidental to the enjoyment as such' does not constitute *development*. You may use the yard at home (but not at work), in general, for such non-commercial purposes as you see fit, provided only that it does not create a *nuisance*.

The perils of change

So before you *develop* your property, or change its use, consider whether or not you need planning permission . . . If you do, then get it . . . If in doubt, consult your local planning authority and/or your architect or surveyor and/or your solicitor.

Check also:

- If you are a tenant, that the proposed alterations or changes will not be in breach of covenant. Many tenants are bound to obtain their landlord's consent before they carry out any building works. You may find, for instance, that while no planning permission is needed in order to make internal changes in your business premises, you cannot do so without permission from your landlords. Ignore the covenant and you may be liable to pay damages – or, at worst, to forfeit your tenancy.

- That you obtain any necessary bye-law consents. Statute apart, local authorities lay down their own rules. These must be complied with. Your local town hall will oblige with details, if required.

- All building bye-laws and regulations must be adhered to. These are designed to ensure adequate and up to date, modern standards. Once again, leave details to your experts, who are paid to study and understand these trying, detailed and complex rules.

Transfers within classes

'In the case of buildings or other land which are used for a purpose of any class specified in an order made by the Minister under this section, the use thereof for any other purpose of the same class shall *not* constitute *development*.' Apart from this rule, it was held that a change from a butcher's shop to a chemist's shop would not be *development* (as already defined), although a change to a fish and chip shop could be. If you are concerned with some change which might move the use out of that of a shop, then you should take expert advice.

Enforcement

Suppose that you should have obtained planning consent but failed to do so. What then? You have unlawfully carried out a development. But you have committed no punishable, criminal offence. Even if you retain the works or continue to carry out the unauthorized use, you commit no offence. But if an enforcement notice is served upon you and you ignore its terms, you do offend against the law. Penalties are laid down.

Where it appears to the local planning authority that there has been a breach of planning control after the end of 1963, then . . . if they consider it expedient to do so having regard to the provisions of the development plan and to any other material considerations, they may serve a notice . . . referred to as an *enforcement notice* . . . requiring the breach to be remedied.

When is there a 'breach of planning control'? If development 'has been carried out . . . without the grant of planning permission required in that behalf . . . or if any conditions or limitation subject to which planning permission was granted have not been complied with'.

Time limits

An enforcement notice may be served within four years from the date of the breach. If you get away with it for longer, you can relax. But 48 months is a long time for even the most sluggish planning authority to forget to take action . . . to lose your file . . . to look before it serves notice . . .

Service of the notice

'An enforcement notice shall be served on the owner and on the occupier of the land to which it relates and on any other person having an interest in that land . . . which . . . is materially affected by the notice.' An enforcement notice must specify:

- The matters alleged to constitute a breach of planning control.
- The steps required by the authority to be taken in order to remedy the breach, i.e. steps for the purpose of restoring the land to its condition before the development took place (or

according to the particular circumstances of the breach) and securing compliance with the conditions or limitations subject to which planning permission was granted.

- The period for compliance with the notice, that is to say the period (beginning with the date when the notice takes effect) within which those steps are required to be taken.

An enforcement notice may require the owner or occupier to demolish or alter any building or works, to discontinue the use of the land or to carry out 'any building or other operations'. It must take effect not less than 28 days after the service of the notice – and it may be withdrawn at any time before it takes effect (happy thought). Notice of withdrawal must be given.

Ignoring the notice

Enforcement notices mean what they say – they give you notice requiring planning rules to be complied with. Unless you propose to comply with the enforcement notice, you must appeal against it. See your lawyer – swiftly.

13

Rating Appeals

- Rates are a major item of expenditure for any trade or business.

- How can you minimize this liability?

Making your appeal

You are entitled to appeal against an assessment, provided that you do so within the time limits laid down. If you have made a proper appeal you may withhold payment of rates in such amount as laid down by statute.

You may appeal on any ground that tends to show that the assessment is incorrect and that the property has been over-valued. If, for instance, you can prove that the area in which your establishment is situated is one in which the standards of service by the local authority are so bad that the value of the property is less than that assessed, then you may be lucky.

Normally, an assessment is lowered because the owner shows that it is out of line with assessments for other similar properties in the area. Alternatively, it is sometimes possible to show that the valuation officer has failed to take into account the disadvantages of the position, age, type or size of the property.

To appeal, you should contact your local Valuation Officer. You could arrange to meet a member of his staff to discuss the situation. Anyway, you could obtain from his office the appropriate advice and form for the making of your appeal (or, to use the technical term, for making a 'proposal' to alter the valuation list).

Written objection

You must make written objection to the Valuation Officer within 28 days after receiving the Valuation Officer's proposal. So do not delay.

After the appeal is lodged, there may then be negotiations with the Valuation Officer which could lead to you withdrawing your objection. Alternatively, you may end up arguing your case before the local Valuation Court. The hearings are generally informal and cost nothing, unless you employ a valuer or other professional to assist you, in which case you will pay his fee. But you are entitled to appear in person if you wish. The court cannot in any event increase your assessment.

By all means consult your solicitor, to see whether he considers that an appeal would be worthwhile. Do not delay.

14

Nuisance

- What are the legal rules on 'nuisance'?

- If you cause a disturbance to your neighbours or they to you, when will the law intervene?

What is 'nuisance'?

You and your neighbours are entitled to reasonable freedom from disturbance. So if the noise, dust, vibration or smoke from premises goes beyond that which an ordinary person would expect to have to put up with as 'part of the give and take of neighbourly life', then it is a *nuisance* in law as well as in fact. The sufferers may then get an injunction from the court – an order restraining you from your unneighbourly behaviour – as well as damages.

The sort of facts which a court would take into account are the nature of the neighbourhood, the degree of the disturbance and whether it extends to unreasonable times of day or night, and whether that disturbance would upset the ordinary, healthy, sensible person.

15

Trespassers

- **What are the rules on trespassers?**
- **And the rights of and your liabilities to people who are on your premises without your permission?**

Using 'reasonable force'

In general, it is for you to decide who may and who may not be on your land. Anyone there without your permission is a trespasser. You may use 'reasonable force' to eject him. And a court may grant you an injunction – an order, restraining him from repeating his wrongful behaviour.

A person has a 'right of way' across your land if he has been granted that right or if he has acquired it 'by prescription' – in general, through enjoying it without interruption and 'as of right' for a period of not less than 20 years. So whether or not your unwanted guests are entitled to be on your property will depend upon whether or not a right of way does in reality exist. If in doubt, you should consult your solicitor.

Own risk

Even people who are entitled to cross your land must not harm your property. Also, while a trespasser in general 'trespasses at his own risk', you may not set a trap for him, hoping to blow his head off with a spring gun, for instance. And if you know that he is likely to be on your land, then Lord Denning has held that you 'owe a legal as well as a humanitarian duty' to take reasonable care for his safety. This rule is especially firmly enforced when the trespasser is a child.

Section 3
Buying, Selling and Insuring

16
A Seller's Checklist

- **Sellers who fall out with the law waste valuable resources.**

- **Conversely, businessmen who survive through sales and know even the most basic legal rules greatly improve their prospects to survive and prosper through times of recession.**

- **So what are the basic rules on selling, as the small businessman should know them?**

Sales law

Whenever you buy or sell, you make a contract, i.e. a legally binding agreement between you and your supplier or customer. In general, the law leaves you to fix your own terms in your own way. That means:

- You may buy in as cheaply and sell as expensively as the market and good business will permit. The Unfair Contract Terms Act does *not* protect the buyer against bad deals.
- Provided that you do not 'discriminate' on grounds of sex or race, you may select your own business relationship, as and when you please – just as your suppliers may select their outlets as they wish.

Exclusions – warranties and guarantees

The law, though, does try to protect buyers. Briefly, the rules are these:

67

- The Sale of Goods Act implies terms into all contracts for the sale of goods – including all business deals – that (in general) goods will be 'of merchantable quality' and 'reasonably suitable for the purpose supplied'.
- Any term in a *business contract* under which the above rights are to be restricted may be declared void by a Court, if it is 'unfair' or 'unreasonable'.
- Any such term in a 'consumer' (or private) contract is void.

So whether an 'exclusion clause' is contained in a guarantee, warranty, order form or other document, when you buy from a business supplier, it may be declared void; but when you sell to the public, it has no effect.

Services

The law relating to the provision of services has been clarified by the *Supply of Goods and Services Act 1982*.

Under Part I of the Act, consumer protection was extended to cover the situation where *goods* are hired or acquired by other means, e.g. where spare parts are supplied in the course of servicing a machine or appliance. In these cases consumers now have a clear statutory right to the normal implied terms that the person providing the goods has title to them, that they are of merchantable quality, fit for their purpose and true to any description applied to them. These rights cannot be excluded by the trader.

Part II of the Act provides that unless it is agreed otherwise, consumers will be able to expect that those who supply *services* will do so with reasonable care, provide the service within a reasonable time and not charge more than a reasonable price.

Representations and trade descriptions

If you induce a customer to buy by making a false statement of fact about the goods, then he may *(i)* reject them and claim his money back; or *(ii)* keep the goods and claim damages to compensate him for the difference between their real value and the value which they would have had, had your statement been true. You may also be guilty, of course, of fraud.

Again: the Trade Descriptions Act makes it a criminal offence to 'apply a false trade description to goods'. Also: to mark goods with a price lower than that at which you are prepared to sell them. So if you mark goods too low through a genuine error, you are not bound to sell them in civil law because you have not 'offered them for sale', but only issued an 'invitation to treat' – inviting members of the public to offer to buy at the price marked. But you could be prosecuted under the Trade Descriptions Act for refusing to sell goods at the price you have marked on them.

Deposits

A deposit is an 'earnest of good faith' – and 'consideration' for keeping goods for the potential buyer. If you take a deposit, then (in the absence of some special agreement to the contrary – such as the 'subject to contract' provision which applies to nearly all contracts for the sale of land), if the buyer does not proceed, you may keep the deposit. Conversely: if no deposit is given, you will not be held bound by a promise to reserve goods for a particular customer.

Breach of contract

If you do sell goods which turn out to be defective, then you are liable to your customer, even though your supplier was in fact at fault. Your customer's remedy is against you – and you may claim contribution or indemnity from your supplier. Remember: your customer is not bound to wait for your supplier's verdict. His contract is with you and you are responsible to him.

If goods are defective, by all means try to induce your customer to accept an exchange or a credit note. But he is not bound to do so. However, if the goods are 'merchantable' and 'fit for the purpose supplied' and you do not wish to oblige a dissatisfied customer, you may certainly refuse a refund. Provided that you have complied with your contract, you are under no legal obligation to oblige your customer.

Cheques

You are not bound to accept a cheque – whether or not it is 'backed' by a banker's card. If a cheque 'bounces' (is dishonoured), then you should normally give 'immediate written notice of dishonour' so that you can sue on the cheque and not on the original debt. But cheques are not 'legal tender'. Be careful to see that the sum payable is set out identically both in the figures and in the writing and that the date is correct.

17

Contracts and Cancellations

- If you make a contract . . . enter into an agreement with a supplier or a customer or anyone else – when can you or the other party cry off and cancel?

- Have you made an effective deal or are there loopholes?

- Are you and the other party still (in law) negotiating – or could you or he force the other party to complete the deal?

Contract checklist

- **Has anyone made a firm offer or are you still at the stage of 'ifs' and 'provided thats'?**

The advert in the paper or the goods on display in the shop window or trade exhibition are not 'offered'. Offers are invited. Equally, an offer that is conditional upon something happening or someone else approving is no offer at all.

- **If there has been an offer, has it been unconditionally accepted?**

If you receive an offer and reply by sending an 'acceptance' subject to your terms, then, if those terms differ substantially from any in the offer, yours is merely 'a counter-offer' and not an 'acceptance'. At that stage, you are still negotiating, even if the other party thinks that the deal is sewn up.

- **Has anyone accepted the 'counter-offer' either formally or, more likely, by delivery of the goods or provision of the services?**

If not, then at any time before action completes the deal, either

71

party (if he knows it) may take advantage of the situation. The buyer may cancel or go elsewhere. The supplier may put up his prices or withdraw the goods or services from the market.

- **Have you agreed on all the main terms?**

If not, then the contract is probably 'too vague to be enforceable'. *Exception:* if you have agreed on the way in which future agreement can be arrived at, thus: 'The price to be agreed or, in the absence of agreement, to be such price as is fixed by the Chairman of the Chamber of Commerce'. Only in the rarest of cases will the Court decide on major terms. *Example:* where contractors do 'extras' on your property with no price agreed in advance. The law then implies a term into the contract that you will pay a 'reasonable price' – that the contractor will be paid on a so-called *quantum meruit* basis.

- **Is the contract one that needs to be made in or evidenced by writing if it is to be effective?**

These exceptional deals include contracts for transfer of an interest in land, for insurance or HP or for the transfer of shares and contracts of guarantee. If it comes within these exceptions then no writing means no deal. Otherwise, the fact that you made your arrangement orally is legally irrelevant.

- **Could you prove that the above main essentials of a contract are all present?**

Writing, of course, is a great help. Most contested cases are eventually decided largely on the documents. But the absence of writing (in all cases other than the above exceptions) does not turn a legally binding contract into a mere 'gentleman's agreement'. In law, if you only have a 'gentleman's agreement', then you or the other party may break it with impunity.

- **Is there any element of illegality in your deal?**

Conspiracies (for example) to contravene the tax laws or contracts for illegal lotteries are void.

- **Have both parties the 'capacity to contract'?**

Minors (aged under 18) can avoid any contracts which are not for 'necessaries' – goods reasonably necessary for them at the time when the deal is done. All minors' business contracts and contracts of loan are void.

- **Can you identify the other contracting party with certainty?**

Take particular care to avoid dealing with or, later, billing a small or rocky company instead of the (hopefully) solvent parent or holding company or outfit with which you believe that you are doing business. Watch out especially for changes in names on note-paper.

- **Are there any 'post-contractual documents', like receipts or delivery notes, which seek to add terms or conditions which were not contained in the original arrangement?**

Initially, these have no effect and can be ignored. They come after the contract. But if either party knows from previous experience that the other side invariably does business only on those terms, then they may become incorporated into future agreements.

- **If you find that you have a binding contract on your hands and it includes exclusion clauses, are those clauses or any of them 'unfair' or 'unreasonable' in all the circumstances of your case?**

If so, then a judge would probably be prepared to declare them void – a power given to him by the Supply of Goods (Implied Terms) Act. This statute also removes the effect of any exclusion clauses dealing with quality ('merchantability') or suitability for use, in contracts made with private buyers ('consumers'). So if you sell goods to the public, you should recognize that these clauses are useless.

- **If you are liable under the contract, can you pass the buck back to anyone else?**

Have you retained a 'right over' against your supplier, so as to obtain an indemnity from him?

- **Have you obtained any necessary insurance – to cover you, perhaps, if you must bear the loss if the goods disappear or are damaged in transit?**

If you cannot answer any of these questions, then the time has probably come to see your solicitor. If the answers are not obvious, then they may be extremely complicated. To save the solicitor's time (and hence your money) remember to take with you all letters, order forms, acceptances or other relevant documents when you see the solicitor, and also, if you can, a typed statement, clearly setting out the facts as you remember them – and, preferably, as you would be prepared to prove them.

18

Must They Have a Second Chance?

- If you sell goods which turn out to be defective, can you insist that your customer accepts a credit note or an exchange?

- Conversely, if contractors mess up a job on your premises, are you entitled to say: 'Once bitten, twice shy – we'll get someone else to put the job right, at the contractor's expense'?

Defective goods

If your goods are defective, your customers are entitled to reject them and to demand the return of their money. If you can get them to accept an exchange or credit, then you are fortunate. But the law says that if you have supplied defective goods, then your customer may demand the return of his money.

Defective services

Equally, if your contractors do not carry out their job for you in a proper and workmanlike manner and with reasonably suitable materials, then they are in breach of their contract with you. You are entitled to damages for breach of contract. And your damage will normally be the cost of putting the job right.

However, you must 'mitigate your loss'. You must keep it to a minimum, as best you reasonably can. And if you do not allow the contractors to remedy their own defects, it could be argued that you did not mitigate your loss as you could have done. So you should certainly consider carefully the contractor's offer before you turn it down.

19

Deductions and Surcharges

- Some suppliers give discounts for prompt payment or impose surcharges for payments made later than a certain date.

- Is this legal?

- Can the small business owner treat his own credit customers in the same way?

Incentives for prompt payment

There is nothing illegal either in trying to provide an incentive to prompt payment or in arranging for interest to be added to accounts which are not paid on time. But while you will not object if your supplier allows you to knock something off his bill, you would have every right to complain if he tries to charge you extra when the surcharge was no part of the original deal.

Surcharges for late payment

If you knew that your supplier did business on the basis that a percentage would be added to accounts paid late, then payment of such surcharges would be enforced by law. But if a supplier simply tries to slam on something extra after the contract has been sewn up, then he is attempting what lawyers call a 'unilateral variation' of a deal – and no court will assist the seller to get money which he was not contractually entitled to receive.

The same rules that apply as between your suppliers and yourself govern your relationship with your customers or clients. If you wish to give discounts, go ahead – but if you want to impose surcharges, include the appropriate term in your contract. And that means in the original arrangement and not merely on your invoice or delivery note.

20

HP and Credit Sales

- **If you sell goods on hire purchase or credit terms, are there any special legal rules that apply?**

- **What is the essence of a sale on those terms?**

Protection for hirer

Under a hire purchase agreement, the buyer hires the goods but is given the right to buy them for an 'option to purchase fee', when all his instalments are duly paid. The terms are agreed between the buyer (who is initially the 'hirer') and the seller (who is the 'owner' – unless he farms out the financing to an HP company or finance house, in which case although the purchase is from him, the lender becomes the 'owner').

Various Hire Purchase Acts lay down a range of protection for the hirer. The agreement must be made in writing and must set out the true terms. If you wish to enter into this sort of business, you should consult your solicitor and make sure that you have proper documentation. You should also watch out for the operation of the Consumer Credit Act.

A credit sale is one on which the goods are sold, so that the buyer becomes the owner immediately, but the seller provides credit, making an interest charge. The purchaser is not nearly as well protected as the buyer on hire purchase. But again, the rules are complicated and you should take specific advice from your lawyer.

21

Mistakes in Marking

- **Are you bound by law to sell goods at the price marked, even if you have made an entirely innocent mistake and left a nought off the ticket?**

In civil law, you are not bound to sell at the price marked. In criminal law, if you refuse to do so you may find that you are prosecuted.

Under the law of contract, when you display goods you are not 'offering' those goods for sale, but merely inviting potential customers to offer to buy them. And the price marked is merely an indication of the amount which you are likely to be prepared to accept. As you have not made an unconditional offer to sell, your customer has no offer to accept. And without offer and acceptance, there is no contract.

It follows that no seller is bound by the price marked on goods – or, for that matter, in a catalogue or in an advertisement. He may refuse to sell at the price marked or at any price or (subject to the law on sex and race discrimination) to any particular customer or at all.

Standing by your mistake

However, the Trade Descriptions Act makes it an offence to apply a false trade description to goods. And it is contrary to the Act to mark goods with a price lower than that at which you are prepared to sell them. So if you do make a mistake, however innocent, in your price marking, then you should stand by that mistake if you reasonably can. While in civil law you can refuse to sell at that price, your customer may report you to the local Consumer Protection Authorities. And if they prosecute, what defence would you have?

At least try to mollify your potential customer. If you refuse to do so, he may report you for a breach of the Trade Descriptions Act. He cannot force you to sell, but a prosecution could cost you even more – in cash and in bad publicity. So in each case, you should weigh the cost of standing by your mistake against the possible consequences of not doing so.

22

An Employee's Authority

- If an employee clearly exceeds the authority you have given him and commits your company to buy an item that you have instructed him not to purchase, is the contract binding on you?

- If so, are you entitled to dismiss the employee?

- Apart from dismissing him, could you have any other legal claims against him?

Binding contract

You will be bound by the employee's contract if it was made either with your actual or apparent or ostensible authority. If you 'held him out' as having the authority to place the order . . . if you 'clothed him with your authority' to make the deal – then it is as binding on you as if his authority was actual.

So you must ask yourself whether or not the supplier should have realized that your employee was not entitled to place the order. If so, then you can refuse to honour it. Otherwise, you are bound.

If you wish to dismiss the employee as a result, then you can only do so summarily, i.e. with neither notice nor pay in lieu, if his misconduct was so serious as to smash his contract of employment. If you are in doubt, consult your solicitor – or pay him his money in lieu of notice 'without prejudice' to your contention that you would be under no legal obligation to do so.

Bearing the loss

If your employee is protected against unfair dismissal, he could bring a claim to an industrial tribunal which would consider whether the sacking was 'fair' in all the circumstances of the case. Was this a sole instance or had he been warned before? Did you listen to his case and give him the right to appeal? Having regard to the employee's past service and record, would a decent employer have behaved as you did – or should the employee have been given another chance?

If you have to proceed with the deal and you suffer loss as a result, you will almost certainly have to bear that loss yourself. Actions against employees claiming damages for the effects of disobeyed instructions are almost unknown.

23

Import, Export and Enforcing Judgments

- If you buy goods from abroad or if you sell overseas, what happens if there is a dispute with your supplier or customer?

- Will our courts intervene or will you have to sue or be sued in another country?

- And if a judgment is obtained by or against you, can it be enforced in the other country or in the UK, as the case may be?

The answers to these questions are usually hugely complicated. If, for instance, you wish to sue overseas, you will have to comply with the rules of the Supreme Court (the High Court of Justice) and get leave to serve your writ in the other country. This will only be possible in specified cases. Often, the answer depends upon the wording of the specific contract and whether the parties have agreed to accept the jurisdiction of a particular court.

Once judgment is obtained, it can only be enforced in the UK or in the other country concerned if the party held to be at fault has assets in that country or if there is a mutual agreement for the 'reciprocal enforcement of judgments'. Recent legislation has helped to ensure that judgments can be enforced with greater ease between EEC countries.

If you are engaged in an import or export business you should discuss your contractual arrangements in detail, with a lawyer expert in this difficult sphere. You should also check on whether you could get help under the Government's various guarantee schemes.

24
Product Liability

- **What is 'product liability'?**

- **And how are the rules likely to change?**

Defective products

Strictly speaking, product liability means the liability of manufacturers and others who put products into circulation for harm done if those products are defective. In practice, the term has come to mean 'strict' or 'no fault' or 'absolute' liability.

If your company manufactures or sells a defective product, legal liability may arise in one of four ways:

- In contract.
- In the tort (or civil wrong) of negligence.
- In crime – under Section 6 of the Health and Safety at Work Act.
- Under the various rules governing an employer's liability to his employees.

Contractual liability only applies to those who are parties to the contract or who benefit by a guarantee or warranty, designed to induce them to buy. But the liability is often strict. Normally, if goods are defective, the buyer may claim damages, irrespective of the cause of the defect.

Contractual rules

Contracts are governed by their terms – they are agreements and the parties can make any deal they like. There are exceptions, though, under the *Supply of Goods (Implied Terms) Act 1973* and the *Unfair Contract Terms Act 1977*, which (in broad terms):

- Remove altogether the effect of exclusion clauses in contracts or in notices, in so far as they seek to exclude or restrict liability for negligence that causes death or personal injury.
- Make totally void any clause that seeks to remove or restrict liability to private buyers ('consumers') in respect of merchantability or fitness for purpose, in contracts for the supply of goods.
- Make such clauses in contracts for the supply of goods to non-consumers of services, or to consumers under business contracts under the seller's own standard written terms and conditions, subject to the test of 'reasonableness'. In other words: they will only be enforceable if and in so far as they are reasonable in all the circumstances of the particular case.
- Leave only exclusion clauses in commercial contracts for the supply of services, not on the supplier's own standard, written terms, to be as unreasonable as the supplier wishes.

If, then, the injured party has a contract with the supplier – or if (as in the case of guarantees or warranties supplied, e.g. with vehicles or electrical appliances) the supplier induces purchase by a 'collateral warranty', then the contractual rules apply. But if the person injured is a stranger to the contract, he must rely upon the rules of negligence.

Negligence

The Thalidomide children, for instance, could not sue the manufacturers in contract because there was no 'privity of contract' between them. So they sued for damages for negligence and therefore had to prove:

- That the goods were defective – which was no problem.
- That the defects had caused damage – again, alas, all too obvious.
- That the suppliers had failed to take all such steps as were reasonable – or had been careless in the steps they took, i.e. that they were 'negligent' – which might well have proved impossible, because the suppliers maintained that they had taken all such precautions as the current state of medical and scientific knowledge would reasonably require.

Because negligence is so difficult to prove and ordinary people cannot finance expensive legal actions, the Royal Commission on Civil Liability (the Pearson Commission) as well as the English and Welsh, and the Scottish Law Commissions all recommend that liability for death or personal injury caused through defective products should be made 'strict', so that sufferers would get damages without proof of fault.

Strict liability

Strict liability exists in most parts of the United States, in West Germany and in France – and the EEC has prepared a revised Draft Directive containing similar provisions. In due course, product liability will arrive in the UK. Meanwhile, business people should look to their insurance – for now and for the future.

It is a criminal offence under Section 6 of the Health and Safety at Work Act for any 'designer, manufacturer, importer or supplier' to fail to take such steps as are 'reasonably practicable' to protect – through research and testing – those who use their articles or substances at work. So those who put defective products into circulation in the UK may not only be sued in a civil court by those who suffer death or personal injury as a result. They may also be prosecuted – and to be acquitted, they must prove that they did that which was 'reasonably practicable'.

There are several defences:

- That all reasonably practicable steps were taken to avoid the hazard.

- That the accused reasonably relied upon research or testing done by others.

- That the customer gave a written undertaking that he would himself carry out research and testing necessary for safety.

- Finally: an employer must take reasonable care for the safety of his employees. If a defective product injures an employee, then the employer may be liable if he has been negligent or in breach of statutory duty, e.g. under the Factories Act. And if he has failed to take such steps as were reasonably practicable to protect employees in this respect, then he may be prosecuted under Section 2 of the Health and Safety at Work Act.

However, if the employee suffers death or personal injury due to a defect in plant or equipment supplied, then under the *Employers' Liability (Defective Equipment) Act 1970* the employer is *deemed* to have been negligent. In this area almost alone in our law, strict liability has arrived. Its extension to all products is only a question of time.

25

Insurance

- **Every business, however small, must carry insurance – for vehicles and people . . . against public and against employers' liability . . . so what are the main legal snags in the insurance world?**

The insurance contract

Whenever you obtain insurance cover, you enter into a contract with the insurers. In consideration of your agreeing to pay the premium, they undertake to provide the specified cover. The terms of the contract are contained in the policy. If you want to know what you are to get for your money, read the policy. If you do not understand it, get it explained.

If you run into trouble over your insurance, then it is useless to ask for legal guidance without showing your policy to your lawyer. He can only advise you on your rights if he knows the terms of the contract – which, we repeat, are in the policy document.

The wise man shops around before he chooses his business supplies, to make sure that he is obtaining the best value available. It is up to him to get what he wants at a fair price. If he pays too much or buys goods which do not suit his purpose, then – assuming that he was not misled by any misrepresentation, and that the goods were not defective – he is out of luck.

Purchasing insurance

Precisely the same principles apply when you purchase insurance. When you purchase insurance cover, it is up to you to make the best bargain you can. The insurance world is highly competitive. The range of policies and cover available is considerable. If you do not get what you bargained for, the fault will be your own.

You can ask individual insurers to quote for the cover you require. You may rely on one company, which you have learned to trust, to supply the insurance you need. Or you may put your affairs in the hands of an insurance broker.

At present, the services of a broker should cost you nothing. They get their commission from the company with which they place your business. It may be that the situation will change before long. But meanwhile, good brokers are worth their weight in gold – and their services come both free and freely to the insured.

Material facts

Usually, before an insurance is made, the proposed insured will find he has to fill in a proposal form. It is absolutely essential that every fact contained in that form should be stated, fully and accurately. Any concealment or misrepresentation of any material fact known to the proposed assured destroys the contract of insurance 'whether of life, fire, or sea or other risk'. Examples:

- If other insurers have declined the proposal, that is a highly material fact.
- If previous claims are not mentioned, the insurers will be able to avoid payment, in the event of a claim.
- Even if the assured is not specifically asked to reveal a fact, he will lose the benefit of the policy if he does not state any fact which would be likely to affect the mind of a prudent insurer considering providing the cover concerned.

'Insurance is a contract of speculation', said Lord Mansfield in a famous judgment.

The special facts upon which the contingent chance is to be computed lie most commonly in the knowledge of the assured only: the underwriter trusts his representation, and proceeds upon confidence that he does not

90

keep back any circumstances in his knowledge, to mislead the underwriter into a belief that the circumstances do not exist. The keeping back of some circumstances is a fraud, and therefore the policy is void.

Although the suppression should happen through mistake, without any fraudulent intention, yet still the underwriter is deceived and the policy is void. . . . The policy would be equally void against the underwriter if he concealed. . . . Good faith forbids either party, by concealing what he privately knows, to draw the other into a bargain from his ignorance of the fact, and his believing the contrary. **⫌**

So (as another judge put it)

❟ Insurance is a contract of the utmost good faith and it is of the gravest importance to commerce that the position should be observed. **⫌**

Fail to observe the position . . . fail to reveal all relevant, material facts within your own knowledge, even if you are not asked to give them . . . conceal, mislead or (worse) defraud – and do not be surprised if the insurers refuse to pay, when you make a claim.

Overvaluation

One fact that is far too often mis-stated is the value of the goods in the premises covered. Under-insure and you may get nothing. Insurers may pay out a proportion but they may be entitled to refuse to do so. Check to make certain that your insurance is adequate.

Conversely, 'excessive overvaluation of the subject matter of an insurance for the purpose of a value policy is a material fact which if not disclosed will render the policy voidable'. Even if you overvalue by mistake, and even if the overvaluation 'does not affect the actual risk', the insurers may avoid payment.

If you suffer loss, then make haste and inform your insurers. Policies often contain conditions requiring notice of loss and details of damage to be given within a stated time and making the policy void if steps are not taken as specified. This is not unreasonable – insurers must be given prompt opportunity to inspect the circumstances of the loss, for their own protection.

Fraud

Fraud on insurers is far too common. Those who deliberately and dishonestly deceive insurers or who attempt to do so may be convicted under the *Theft Act 1968*. Those who set light to their own buildings in order to obtain insurance monies are guilty of arson. Many who have been caught are now in prison.

Fraudulent exaggeration of a claim (as where a vehicle owner 'piles on the agony', adding previous damage to that caused in an accident) is not only criminal but fully entitles insurers to repudiate liability.

In one case where the assured acted fraudulently in relation to insurance policies and failed to disclose this when applying for further policies, a court held that he had concealed a material circumstance. Once the assured has a bad name, he keeps it – and others are entitled to know. Good faith, a good name and complete honesty generally lead to prompt payment of claims and a satisfactory relationship with the insurers.

Choosing your insurance company

The converse applies. It is worth choosing reputable, well established insurers, who pay promptly – even if their premiums are higher (which is far from inevitable). Often, the best insurers will meet claims even though they could, if they wished, avoid them on some technical ground – such as late notification or accidental non-disclosure. There are laws curbing 'fly by night' insurers. But there is still a good deal to choose between the companies – as well as between the policies they offer.

Choose well, then. . . . Make your choice with care. . . . Tell the truth, the whole truth and nothing but the truth to your insurers . . . and your insurance policies should enable you to sleep well at night. But ignore the legal snags and you will have paid your money for nothing.

Section 4

Money and Debts

26

You and Your Bank

- Whenever you make an arrangement with your bank, you enter into a contract.

- So what are your rights against that bank – and what are the bank's powers against you?

- How can you guard against dud cheques?

Borrowing money

The bank's rights against you and your rights against the bank depend on the law of contract. Whenever you lend money to the bank or – alas, more likely – whenever you borrow from it, you enter into a contract of loan. The lender – you or the bank, as the case may be – lays out cash in return for a promise that it will be repaid on agreed terms.

Repaying a loan on demand Theoretically, in the absence of agreement to the contrary, every loan, including one made by a bank, is repayable on demand. In practice, an advance is normally made for an agreed period. The manager says, perhaps: 'We will review in six months'. The bank is bound by that. And an efficient manager notes the agreement in his records.

If an inefficient manager makes an incorrect record and you get asked to repay before your time has expired, then protest. It is extremely unlikely that you will have anything to worry about.

Once the agreed period has passed, then – again in theory – you could be required to repay your debt. But if you are dealing with one of the big four banks – or with most of the smaller ones – it is extremely unlikely that your securities will be sold or the bank's

95

image jeopardized by starting legal proceedings against you. You will almost certainly be asked to make your own proposals for repayment. The bank is not bound to accept them – but you will find it so reluctant to take stronger remedies that if your proposals have substance at all, they will almost certainly be accepted.

Overdrafts   Anyway, your right to an overdraft depends on the bank's agreement, so it is up to you to hammer out the best arrangement you can – and to get your manager to agree to grant you the facilities you want for the period you require them.

Not only are you entitled to negotiate, so as to get your loan for the maximum period – or, for that matter, so as to have that period extended – but you should also try to get the interest charged at the lowest rate possible.

Big industrial and commercial borrowers are likely to get the lowest rates of interest and the private individual may have to pay the most. But it is still much cheaper to borrow from one of the big four – Barclays, Lloyds, Midland or National Westminster – and all their branches – or even from most of the merchant banks – than it is to get your money through a hire purchase company.

Interest charges   The reason for this, of course, is that the banks normally charge interest only on the amount of the loan outstanding, so that your repayments are taken into account – while finance companies charge interest on the full amount of the loan, so that your repayments are not taken into account, no matter how much has been repaid.

Anyway, what matters is to make the best contract you can with your bank. If you are a reliable, regular customer whose affairs are well regulated, your bank manager will do his best to help you, even in hard times when credit is short.

Exercising power   Now suppose that you cannot comply with your promise – perhaps to reduce your overdraft at an agreed rate. Theoretically, your bank manager could force you to pay. Or maybe you have had to lodge shares as security for the loan – the bank could sell them so as to recover its money.

Happily, banks seldom exercise the powers they have. The

borrower generally gets more leeway than the law could force the bank to grant.

So – to summarize – your rights against your bank depend on the arrangement you come to with your bank manager. You will be entitled to your agreed facilities – and once granted the bank will not be free to refuse those facilities to you. The bank must take care, for instance, not to bounce your cheques when there is money in your account or available in your agreed facilities, sufficient to meet the amount of that cheque.

For your part, you must pay the interest and repay the capital in accordance with your agreement – and if you cannot do so, then you must make your peace with your bank manager as best you can.

Luckily, provided that the small businessman can make some sensible proposal, he is unlikely to be in trouble. So do not panic. The bank makes its living out of the interest paid by its clients. It is in fierce competition with other banks. And while clients' rights are minimal in theory, in practice they are in a much stronger position than the manager's firm letters would suggest.

Dud cheques

How can you avoid the perils of dud cheques? Remember the following:

- Cheques are not 'legal tender'. You are not bound to accept them. You are entitled to insist upon payment by cash or banker's order. Alternatively (in appropriate cases) you may decline to deliver equipment or to provide services (as the case may be) until the cheque has been cleared.
- By all means insist that the giver of the cheque provide you with his name and address and with some means of identification – or, better still, only accept a cheque if it is backed by a banker's card.
- Find out whether, in your particular circumstances, you could insure against bad debts due to dishonoured cheques. The

97

premium may not be worth paying. But an enquiry costs nothing.

- Make firm rules for your staff as to when and from whom cheques may be accepted and when and whether authority should be obtained at a higher level.

- If a cheque for a large sum is dishonoured, inform your solicitors immediately – and if you suspect dishonesty, inform the police.

If a cheque does 'bounce', then unless it has been stopped by the drawer (that is, by the giver) you must give him immediate written notice of dishonour. In practice, it is far swifter and less expensive to sue the drawer of a dishonoured cheque for the amount of the cheque than it is to claim damages for breach of contract, arising out of the transaction for which the cheque was given. There is seldom any good legal answer to a claim on a cheque – but there are many gates open to those sued for broken contracts.

Credit cards and cheque guarantee cards

Make sure that you and your staff are fully conversant with the differences between credit cards and cheque guarantee cards. The main point to remember is that a credit card may be used on its own to purchase goods and services, but a cheque guarantee card may only be used to guarantee a cheque up to the limit set by the bank.

To make matters more complicated, some cards, like the *Barclaycard*, may be used both as a credit card and as a cheque guarantee card. You and your staff should be familiar with the conditions of use of the main cards from the banks and credit card companies and should be careful to follow the procedures laid down.

27

Debt Collecting

- **If you are owed money and cannot get it, what should you do?**

- **With interest rates so high, you cannot afford to allow debts to remain outstanding longer than absolutely necessary.**

If you are owed money, you are entitled to be paid either when the agreed date for payment arrives or, in the absence of agreement, on demand. So if the due date has passed or your demand has been made and you are still owed your money, what should you do?

Weighing up the tactics

First, consider tactics. If you move in too fast, then you may destroy your debtor, while patience could bring in the money you are owed. Consider: is your debtor playing for time because of a genuine, temporary, cash-flow problem – in which case, to sue would be a mistake. Or should you jump in with both feet in the hope of getting hold of what little money may be available?

If you do need the help of the law, then you must sue for your money. Once you have judgment (and become a 'judgment creditor'), the law provides a series of possible methods of enforcing your judgment (against the 'judgment debtor'). For instance:

- You may *distrain* on the debtor's property. If you are owed rent, you will send in the bailiffs. Otherwise, the Court will do so. They will take hold of property belonging to the debtor and sell it in whole or partial payment of the judgment debt.

- You may apply for an *oral examination* of the judgment debtor as to his means.

- You may apply for a *charging order* on the debtor's house or other 'real' (as opposed to personal) property.

- If the debtor has a job, then you should apply for the *attachment* of his earnings. Then his employer will deduct a specified sum from his pay packet and pay it into the Court for you.

- You may make him *bankrupt* – or, in the case of a company, try to have it wound up.

In each case, of course, you have to weigh the likelihood of success against the cost of the proceedings. If the amount of the debt is small and the debtor has a possible defence – or if the debtor is likely to be a 'man of straw' – then you may be better off to write off the debt, rather than to chase the debtor.

Remember, too, that the Court will not normally grant you any order for legal costs against the debtor if you issue a summons in cases of debts under £500. Anyway, if in doubt you should consult your solicitor and take and follow his advice. Or put the collection into the hands of a specialized agency.

28

Insolvency and Dissolution

- How do you close down your business – or part of it?
- What are the legal rules on insolvencies – the bankruptcy of an individual or the liquidation of a company?

Bankruptcy

The rules on bankrupcty are laid down by the Bankruptcy Acts – which are carefully designed to make it unpleasant for the man who too readily attempts to rid himself of his liabilities. For instance, no undischarged bankrupt may lawfully obtain credit for £10 or more without revealing his undischarged state. The object, of course, is to prevent people from getting rid of one accumulation of creditors so as to start right away on acquiring another.

Then, once you are bankrupt, you may not find it too easy to get discharged. You will be expected to pay off your debts as best you can and as swiftly as possible. You will not simply be able to heave your worries out the window and keep anything you earn for yourself. The idea will be to see just how much you can repay and how swiftly.

Nor will you have much joy in concealing your money or transferring your home into your wife's name. 'Fraudulent preferences' are common. And those who commit them are highly unpopular with the law.

If you fraudulently convey your property, conceal yourself, abscond to avoid paying your debts or fail to satisfy a judgment of the court, you commit an 'act of bankruptcy'. You may then have a bankruptcy notice served on you. A receiving order will be made and an Official Receiver or Trustee in Bankruptcy put in control of all your property.

Dissolving

What, then, of partnerships? A partnership for a fixed period will automatically be dissolved when that period expires. It can be revived. But otherwise it is dead. Again, if you enter into a particular venture with others, with a view to common profit, when that venture comes to an end, so does the partnership. Most common of all are partnerships of no fixed duration. These are called 'partnerships at will'. Any partner can dissolve them at any time by serving a notice on his fellow partners. The firm dissolves when the notice says that it is to come to an end.

Application of partner The court can dissolve a partnership on the application of any of the partners, in certain specified circumstances. The most common is where 'any partner has behaved in a way calculated prejudicially to affect the carrying on of the partnership business' (in other words, there is a battle between the partners), or when the partnership business can only be continued at a loss.

To some extent, the procedure in a particular dissolution will be laid down in a partnership deed or agreement, if there is one. If you have one, look at it. If you do not, then get one. It is not at all clever to operate a firm without having worked out on paper the arrangements between the members, including what is to happen if the marriage has to be dissolved.

Winding up companies

As for companies, they may be wound up voluntarily or compulsorily. If the directors deliver to the Registrar of Companies, not less than five weeks before the passing of a resolution by the shareholders to dissolve the corporation, a statutory declaration confirming that the company will pay all its debtors in full within 12 months of the start of the winding up, then there is a *members' voluntary winding up*. The liquidator will be appointed and controlled by the shareholders.

If there can be no statutory declaration, the voluntary winding up may be a *creditors' winding up*. The day following the resolution, a creditors' meeting is called and a liquidator appointed. But if the shareholders and creditors cannot agree on what is to happen to the business, it is the creditors who will appoint the liquidator and control him.

In either event, the court may step in and order the winding up to proceed under its supervision. But if you cannot pay your debts, the most unpleasant result is likely to be a compulsory winding up. Amongst the reasons why a court can wind up a company are that it is unable to pay its debts or if the court is of the opinion 'that it is just and equitable that the company should be wound up'.

When are you solvent?

We all live on credit and many of us could be thoroughly 'solvent' if we sold off all our assets. So when is a company 'unable to pay its debts'? In general:

- If a creditor who is owed more than £200 has demanded payment but has gone three weeks without being satisfied.
- If execution is levied in an attempt to realize money owing under a judgment, and that execution is returned unsatisfied.
- If a court is satisfied that the company is unable to pay its debts, having regard to 'the contingent and prospective liabilities of the company', insolvency is then apparent.

The right people to advise you, if you have a mind to declaring your own insolvency, no matter how you operate your business, are your own expert advisers – your solicitor and your accountant. They will know details of your own personal arrangements and finances and be able to tell you whether, in their view, you are likely best to head off disaster by heading for the Bankruptcy Court. Before you do so, check on the likely cost – it may be far higher than you expect. A debtor against whom a receiving order has been made may make a proposal for a *composition* in satisfaction of his debts or for a *scheme of arrangement* of his affairs. Under a scheme of arrangement the debtor hands over his assets to a trustee. A composition enables the debtor to keep hold of his assets whilst promising to pay his creditors a sum proportionate to the amount of the debt. Both procedures require the approval of the Court. A further and more common procedure is available in the County Court where the Registrar will get together all the judgment debts against you and make appropriate orders.

No businessman should regard insolvency as an easy way out of trouble. However hard the winter, if your business is gone, the chances of sunshine in the spring are pretty remote.

29

Closing Down - Your Checklist

- **If you do close your business, you must look at the problems with your premises, your employees, your suppliers and your creditors.**

- **What effect will they have on you?**

- **Are you a freeholder or a tenant?**

If you own the freehold, then you are fully entitled to sell it, as and when you wish, provided that you can find a buyer. If you are short of cash, you may still be able to sell and then to lease back the premises from the buyer. But there is no legal reason why you should not dispose of your asset.

- **Are you a tenant?**

If so, then carefully examine your lease or tenancy agreement to see whether there is any term affecting assignment or sub-letting. These may be absolutely forbidden – in which case you are in the hands of your landlords. They may waive the prohibition, probably in return for payment, but possibly with some relief if your business is in trouble and you can find an assignee or sub-tenant in a stronger business position.

- **Do you need your landlord's consent to assignment or sub-letting?**

If so, the law implies a term that such consent shall not be unreasonably withheld. If you find a responsible and solvent assignee or sub-tenant who can provide adequate references, you *should* be in the clear. But your landlord may make life difficult for you by delaying his approval.

- **Have you given any person a guarantee?**

If you are the original tenant under a lease, the landlords may have a come-back against you if your assignee does not comply with the covenants. So *you* may need a personal guarantee from an individual before you assign to a limited liability company.

- **Check the curious rules on redundancy.**

If you make an employee redundant, then you will have to find half the redundancy pay out of the reserves of your business (or, in the case of an individual trader, out of his own assets). If you put your company into liquidation, then the entire redundancy pay comes from public funds – and the Revenue provides in the liquidation for the half which the company should have paid – but its claim goes into the pool along with other non-preferential creditors.

- **Are you selling the business?**

If so, then any employee who takes a job with the purchasers is not redundant – nor is an employee who refuses the same or a similar position with the new boss. Otherwise, any employee put out of work because of your business decision is redundant and is entitled to redundancy pay even if he obtains other work immediately, assuming:

1 That he has worked for you for at least 2 years.
2 That he normally worked at least 16 hours a week, or 8 hours after 5 years' continuous service.
3 That the employee is above the age of 20 and below retirement age (65 years if a man, 60 if a woman).

- **How much redundancy pay would you have to find?**

That depends on the length of service of each employee and his remuneration. Check with your solicitor, accountant or the local office of the Department of Employment.

- **Have you outstanding orders with suppliers, for goods or for equipment?**

If these are already purchased, you may dispose of them as you wish. But even if they have not been delivered, the closing of a business or branch or unit will not give you any right to cancel orders.

- **All contractual documents should be handed to your solicitors.**

They may find loopholes – maybe some element of a binding contract was missing. Perhaps your unconditional order was not 'accepted' by the supplier, who only agreed to deliver on terms substantially different from yours (hence making a 'counter-offer').

- **If the deal is a firm one, you have no right to cancel because you have decided to go into a different line of business, to move your premises, to sell or to close down.**

If you refuse to accept delivery, you will have broken the contract and your supplier will be entitled to damages. Therefore:

1 Can you induce your supplier to let you off the hook – for the sake of goodwill; or because of your difficulties in paying for the goods if they are delivered?

2 If you are selling, can you get the assignee to take over your obligations?

3 If you are going to have to pay damages, then check on the profit which your supplier will not now make on the deal. But can he mitigate his loss by selling elsewhere? If so, then he must do so. *Note:* there is no need for a term in your contract with the supplier giving him a right to damages. Such a term is inevitably implied into a contract for the supply of goods or services of any sort, in the absence of some agreement to the contrary.

- **Have you consulted your solicitor and accountant, so as to sort out all the legal and tax angles (including possible tax losses)?**

It is vital that you should know both the strengths and the weaknesses of your position.

- **Are your records in order?**

Anyone who considers buying your business will wish to inspect the books and to know the precise trading position.

- **If you close down the business, then you will have to make your peace with the creditors.**

Among factors affecting the strength of your bargaining position will be the following:

1 Liquidity of the business.
2 Whether it has been trading as a separate company or part of a major enterprise.
3 The extent of the limitation of its liability – as opposed to the existence of personal guarantees from you, your family or others.
4 The reasonableness of any offers which you can make to those who are owed money.
5 The answers to the problems posed above.

Finally, thanks to the Employment Protection Act, watch out for two additional rights given to employees:

- If any of your employees are members of recognized independent trade unions, be sure to give as much advance warning as you can of any intended redundancy (whether or not you are intending to close your business). You must also inform the Department of Employment as well as any relevant trade union of any major proposed redundancies of ten or more people at any one 'establishment'.
- Failure to comply with the duty to consult a trade union will give that union the right to apply to an Industrial Tribunal for repayment to its members the sum equal to that which he would have received during the period when consultation would have taken place. Failure to nofity the Department may result in a fine of up to £400 or loss of up to 10 per cent of the redundancy rebate.

- An employee may now get up to eight weeks pay and six weeks holiday pay as well as any other money owed, either as a preferential debt or (when the employer's kitty is empty) from the Redundancy Fund. Details from the Department of Employment, your solicitor, or the Advisory, Conciliation and Arbitration Service (ACAS).

Section 5

Your Staff

30

The Employee's Rights

- **What are the rights of the individual employee – and his duties?**
- **What can you do if he gives no notice?**
- **Can he compete with you when he leaves your employ?**
- **Are you entitled to poach staff from other employers?**

The normal rule in business contracts is: they bind both sides or neither. If the deal is binding on you, then it will be binding on the other party – otherwise, not at all. Theoretically, contracts of employment are the same. But while an employer who breaks the rules may be in trouble, an employee (for curious reasons, which we will now trace) normally escapes scot-free.

As an employer, it is vital that you should recognize your powerlessness, if only so that you do not waste time and money on consulting lawyers or instituting proceedings which will be useless. As an employee on the other hand, you may be grateful for the benevolence of the law. So here is a collection and summary of the rules – some of which have been previously covered in this book and some of which are new.

Notice

Employers are bound to give:

- Such period as is agreed between employer and employee.
  Or:

113

- In the absence of agreement, such notice as is reasonable in all the circumstances. And:
- In any event, not less than the statutory minimum: to the employee, 1 week after 1 month's service; 2 weeks after 2 years' service; 3 weeks after 3 years' service; and so on up to 12 weeks after 12 years' service.

If an employer does not give proper notice, then he dismisses 'wrongfully'; and the employee can prove his loss – which (in broad terms) is the remuneration he would have received during the period of notice, minus anything that he actually manages to earn during that period.

When the employee gives no notice

If an employee does not give proper notice, i.e. agreed notice or otherwise the statutory minimum 7 days, he has broken his contract of service. But if his employer sues for damages, he will get none – because he cannot prove his loss. In practice, it is impossible to show how much the premature departure of an employee costs. Reasons:

- The cost of finding a replacement would have been incurred, even had the employee given his proper notice.
- Profits depend not only on the absence (or presence) of an employee but on everything from the vagaries of trade to the peculiarities of the weather.
- If an employee leaves early, you do not have to pay him his money – and you may even make a profit on the deal.

Unfair competition

So, in practice, an employee can leave without giving any notice and you can do nothing about it. He may then set up in competition either on his own or for your top competitor. The only restraints on an ex-employee's freedom are:

- He may not take with him any property that belongs to you – including the company car, the samples, stationery or stamps.
- Theoretically, he may not steal your secrets or confidential information – but if he does not take documents, it is rarely possible to prove the theft of ideas.
- He may not compete against you if there is a valid, binding restraint clause in his contract of service.

Poaching staff

Just as an employee may take with him his skill, know-how, knowledge and contacts when he goes, so your competitors are entitled to entice your top employees away from your service. There is no close season for the poaching of staff. Exceptions:

- It is improper to 'induce a breach of contract', i.e. to procure an employee to leave without giving his proper notice. But try proving it. (*Note:* it is not good enough that the employee eventually left without giving notice and went to a competitor – you have to prove that the contractual breach was caused by the competitor.)
- Your competitor may not trespass on your property by sending his scouts actually on to your premises.

Remedies

If you can prove that your ex-employee has taken a job in breach of a reasonable (and hence enforceable) restraint clause, or that he is using your mailing list, for example, then the Court may award two remedies:

- An injunction, to restrain any continuation of the improper practice. And/or:
- Damages, to compensate you for the loss you have suffered.

If your employee leaves, check his contract (or the written particulars) to see if it contains a restraint clause. If there is competition but no clause you will have to beat it as best you can. If you do find a restraint clause and you regard your ex-employee as being in breach of it, consult your solicitor. But if the employee has merely failed to give proper notice, do not waste your time or money on going to your lawyer.

Conversely, if you wish to leave your company, you may lose goodwill and any hope of a reference if you do not give proper notice – but the chances of your employers having any legal rights worth enforcing against you are negligible. And if you wish to compete, look at your contract or written particulars; if there is no restraint clause, rejoice; if there is a clause which is unreasonably wide, you will be lucky; if in doubt, consult your solicitor.

31

Appointment and Recruitment - Your Employment Contract Checklist

- When did you last check the basic terms of your employees' contracts? Remember: within 13 weeks of the start of their employment or four weeks of any change, they are entitled to written particulars of their main terms of service.

There are some areas which require special attention:

- **Mobility clauses** – giving employers (where appropriate) the right to require employees to change *(i)* their place of work; and/or *(ii)* their hours of work.
- **Job title** – especially *(i)* for a woman employee, because after maternity leave she is entitled to return to 'her job'; and *(ii)* for flexibility – once again, in case movement becomes necessary.

Among those clauses which you should most carefully consider, but which are not required, are the following:

- **Moonlighting** – is an employee entitled to do other work, without your consent? The law will imply a term that the

117

employee will not compete with you or make it impossible for him to do his job – but otherwise, only an express clause can make moonlighting improper.

- No matter what is in your contracts, an employee's *inventions* belong to him unless *(i)* the employer buys the invention or a licence to use it; or *(ii)* the employee is specifically employed to invent, e.g. on R&D, and the invention is one which he should reasonably be expected to invent in the course of that employment. If the employee is employed to invent, say so – clearly and with sensible detail.

- **Medical examinations** should be required, at your request – not only to avoid unwarranted absenteeism for alleged sickness, but also (and more positively) to enable you to do everything reasonably possible to ensure the health of all your employees, including your managers.

- **Search** clauses are advisable where theft is likely – but, of course, do not remove the requirement to get consent to search a person or property at the time.

- **Restraint** clauses are the only hope of avoiding competition by ex-employees – but these should be drafted by experts because each will only be upheld if it is 'reasonable'.

Other crucial reminders:

- Disciplinary and dismissal procedures must be set out – or made reasonably accessible to employees. The two procedures merge one into the other but should be kept separate. The primary object of disciplinary procedures is to achieve good behaviour and to avoid the need for dismissals.

- **Suspension** is necessary to avoid hasty decisions and to allow investigations – normally, without loss of pay. It is also useful, on occasions, without pay, as part of a disciplinary procedure.

- **Maternity** notices are now complicated. They do not have to be set out in any specific form and certainly not in the employment particulars. But the procedure should be clear, agreed (where appropriate) with unions and full information given to the employees concerned at the appropriate time.

118

- Although you have 13 weeks within which to provide the particulars, you should in fact provide them whenever possible before the employee starts work. Give the employee the opportunity to read them and to ask questions. He cannot then complain afterwards that he did not know the terms of his employment.

- No employee is bound to sign his terms of service – conversely, the fact that he fails to do so in no way affects their validity. But do obtain signatures whenever reasonably practicable, so that you clearly show that the employee received (and, if possible, read) them.

- **Union procedures** – including any union membership agreement (commonly but imprecisely referred to as a 'closed shop agreement') – should be specified.

- Finally, if you intend to change your particulars, do consult in advance – with unions and (please) with your own partners and colleagues.

32

Holiday Entitlement

- **How long must an employee be with you before he is entitled to holidays or holiday pay?**

Holiday entitlement depends primarily upon the employee's own contract of employment. The law leaves it up to employer and employee to make their own terms. Curiously, statute only gives women and young people working in factories an absolute entitlement, even to the 'statutory' holidays.

However, if any employee is covered by Wages Council Regulations, he will be entitled to those *minimum* holiday rights set out in the Order concerned.

33

Non-manual Workers– and Payment by Cheque

- When are you entitled to pay an employee by cheque or otherwise than in cash?

Who is a non-manual worker?

You must pay a manual worker in cash, unless he has agreed in writing to accept that payment by some other method.

Payment to non-manual employees may be by any method agreeable to them and to their employer. In practice, it is sometimes difficult, though, to know who is a 'manual worker' – or, to use the term in the *Truck Act 1831*, who is an 'artificer'.

The test applied by the courts is whether the 'real and substantial part of the employment' is manual or whether manual work is 'merely incidental and accessory to' the real employment. A worker may still be 'manual' even though he sometimes serves customers. But a cashier or sales assistant is not a 'manual worker'. Other people who have been held by courts *not* to be 'manual workers' include: research workers whose efforts involve manual labour, hairdressers (even though they work with their hands) and even bus conductors and van drivers.

In the spring of 1983 the Government put forward new proposals for updating the law relating to payment of wages. So watch out for legislation designed to make the spread of cashless pay easier.

34

Discrimination

- **What are the rules on pay and sex discrimination?**

Equal pay

Men and women are entitled to equal pay for equal work – you must not discriminate against a woman by paying her less for work which is either the same or assess on the same basis. This was laid laid down in the *Equal Pay Act 1970* and has been amended and strengthened by the *Sex Discrimination Act 1975*, so that a 'non-discrimination' clause is now implied into every employee's contract.

Discrimination

It is unlawful to discriminate against an employee because he is a man or woman or because he or she is married. This applies to selection, appointment, training, promotion and dismissal alike. Discrimination remains permitted on the ground that a person is unmarried.

It is unlawful to discriminate against an employee in any of the above respects (appointment, etc.) because of his or her race, nationality, colour or ethnic or national origin. To some extent, these definitions have yet to be judicially defined.

It is unlawful to discriminate against an employee because he wishes to join or not to join, to take part in or to keep out of the activities of a trade union. This area of law has been further developed and made even more complex by the *Employment Acts 1980 and 1982.*

Infringement of rights So important are these rights that their infringement not only gives the person discriminated against the right to bring an action to an industrial tribunal, but if he is dismissed on grounds of discrimination, the normal qualifying periods for unfair dismissal protection do not apply. In addition, if he can obtain a certificate from a trade union official that he has been dismissed on grounds of discrimination, the tribunal may (and very occasionally does) order that he be kept in the employer's employment until the unfair dismissal case is heard.

In addition, the statutory provision which enables a tribunal to order that the employee be reinstated in his job was mainly introduced so as to make discrimination more expensive.

With the doubling of the qualifying period for unfair dismissal protection, the discrimination exceptions became potentially more important, but there is no evidence that their use has increased. Indeed, it has proved very difficult to establish discrimination on grounds of sex and almost impossible on grounds of race. This sort of discrimination clearly exists, but is difficult to prove.

There are also several important exceptions to the rules. You may, for instance, discriminate on grounds of sex where 'sex is an essential qualification for the job'.

Changes in the law

There are likely to be significant changes in the law relating to sex and race discrimination in the near future, some of them designed to bring UK law into line with the rules in the EEC.

Important new rules in the parliamentary pipeline also relate to sex discrimination and equal pay. A new equal pay order will provide for women to obtain equal pay for work of equal value even if there are no men carrying out the work and no job evaluation study has been made.

35

Women, Children and Foreigners

- **What special rules should you know, as they affect the employment of women, children and foreigners?**

Women and children first

In most respects, men and women are treated in employment on an equal basis. Indeed, the Equal Pay Act and the Sex Discrimination Act do their best to ensure that no one, man or woman, is discriminated for or against on the grounds of his or her sex. Residual protection remains for 'women and young persons' who work in factories. But there are no special rules to protect women in shops or offices.

In brief, no schoolchild may work in a factory nor anywhere else until he has reached the age of 14. For the last two years before leaving school, he must not be employed before the end of school hours on any day on which he is required to attend school, nor before 6 in the morning or after 8 in the evening on any day, nor for more than 2 hours on any day on which he is required to attend school nor for more than 2 hours on a Sunday. Nor must he 'lift, carry or move anything so heavy as to be likely to cause injury to him'.

Still, there are exceptions. You should check with your local authority to find out what bye-laws apply in your particular area.

Foreigners

Foreigners who are domiciled within the EEC are treated for employment purposes on the same basis as UK nationals. But strict rules in general forbid the employment of other foreigners, unless they have work permits. Usually, you cannot employ a foreigner to do a job unless you can prove that you cannot get a British resident to do it. In times of high unemployment, these rules tend to be enforced with more precision than compassion. If you have trouble in any particular case and you cannot sort it out on behalf of your actual or proposed employee, consult your Member of Parliament who may intervene with the Home Office on your behalf.

Work permits

The procedure for obtaining a work permit depends upon the status of the prospective employee. Applications must be made on Form OW1 by the employer. These forms are available at a Professional and Executive Recruitment Office (PER), Jobcentre or employment office. An application should be made at least eight weeks before the permit is required.

Applications relating to workers abroad or already in approved employment, other than as a trainee, should be returned to the nearest PER office, Jobcentre or employment office (see your telephone book). Applications relating to workers already in the UK but not in approved employment must be sent to the Home Office, Immigration and Nationality Department, Lunar House, Wellesley Road, Croydon, Surrey.

36

Employing the Disabled

- **When must the small business employ at least one registered disabled person?**

The duty to *give employment to a quota of registered disabled persons* applies only to employers who *in accordance with their normal practice and apart from transitory circumstances would have not less than 20 persons in their employment.* In other words, if you have fewer than 20 people on your payroll, you are not bound to employ anyone who is registered as disabled.

If you expand your business so as to have 20 or more people, you will still exclude anyone whose employment *ordinarily involves less than 10 hours weekly service.* Remember: a *part-timer* for the purposes of unfair dismissal protection is a person who *normally works* less than 16 hours a week or 8 hours after 5 years' continuous service. But for the *Disabled Persons (Employment) Act 1944*, and the Regulations made under it, part-timers who work 10 hours or more are included.

However, where an employee works not less than 10 but not more than 30 hours a week, then he is counted as 'one half of a unit'; but once he works for 30 hours, then he is treated in the same way as any other full-timer.

Statutory obligations apart, of course, it is important to help disabled people where you can, especially in periods of high recession and unemployment like the present. But in your position as a very small business, the law will not require you to do so.

37

Homeworkers and Outworkers

- **What are your obligations to homeworkers and outworkers?**

The first question to ask is: Do I 'employ' the person? If he is self-employed, then he has no protection against (for instance) unfair dismissal or redundancy. Nor are payments subject to PAYE or National Insurance contributions. If in doubt, consult your solicitor or your accountant.

Anyway, you should do what is 'reasonably practicable' to protect outworkers and homeworkers against hazards caused by your work. Even if they are not 'employees' and covered by Section 2 of the Health and Safety at Work Act, they are certainly 'affected by your undertaking' and protected by Section 3.

Anyway, small business people who employ people in their own homes or other premises should draw up careful agreements, preferably prepared by solicitors, so as to make the relationship and the obligations as clear as possible. This should avoid disputes, not only between the parties, but also with the Revenue and with the Customs and Excise.

38

Maternity Notices

- **What notice must a woman give if she wants to get her maternity pay and leave?**
- **And when is she entitled to time off for ante-natal care?**

Maternity pay and leave

The *Employment Act 1980* requires a woman to give notice when she wishes to obtain maternity pay, at least 21 days before her absence begins 'if reasonably practicable'. She must do so in writing, if her employer so requests, or if she wants maternity leave. In addition, for leave, the following notices are required:

- Not less than 49 days after the week or date of confinement, the employer may give the mother a written request to confirm her intention to return. She must do so in writing within 14 days of receiving the request, or as soon thereafter as is reasonably practicable.
- She must give written notice to her employers at least 21 days before exercising her right to return.

In addition, an employer with five or fewer employees* need not reinstate an employee after maternity leave, where it is not 'reasonably practicable' for him to do so. The mother also loses her right to return if she 'unreasonably refuses' suitable alternative employment offered to her by an employer of any size.

---

*Part-timers are included in the minimum. So if a business employs more than five people, including part-timers, the usual maternity leave provisions apply.

Note: even to qualify for maternity pay an employee must give notice to her employer that she will be away 'due to pregnancy or confinement' where reasonably practicable at least 21 days before her departure. This notice need only be in writing if the employer so requests.

- Wise employers request written notice – both in the employee's contract of employment or written particulars and as part of normal maternity procedure.
- Wise employees give timely written notice both for maternity pay and leave and keep copies.

Maternity pay remains 6 weeks at 9/10ths of the employee's normal pay minus the maximum current maternity allowance. Maternity leave normally begins not earlier than 11 weeks before the date of the expected confinement and the employee must return not less than 29 weeks after the birth, unless she is not well enough to come back, in which case she may stay away an extra 4 weeks.

Ante-natal care

Employees are also entitled to 'reasonable' time off for ante-natal care. The employee must bring, at the employer's request, a certificate of pregnancy. Also, the employer is entitled to a note, showing the time and place of each appointment, other than the first.

Unlike the right to maternity pay or leave, though, the employee does not have to show any minimum qualifying period of employment in order to claim her ante-natal time off work. She is entitled to it from the day her employment begins.

39

Sick Pay and Absenteeism – the New Rules

- **If an employee is ill, what are his rights to sick pay?**

Categories of sick pay

A sick employee has three possible sources of payment: occupational sick pay (OSP) from his employer; statutory sick pay (SSP) – also payable by his employer; and sickness benefit from the Department of Health and Social Security.

An employee's right to OSP will depend on the terms of his contract of employment. If there is no express term in the contract, then, in certain cases, a right to sick pay may be *implied* by previous conduct. This is a difficult area of law and, if in doubt in any particular case, you should consult your solicitor.

Statutory Sick Pay (SSP)

The scheme came into force in April 1983. In bringing in SSP, the Government transferred the administrative burden from the DHSS to individual employers – large and small. Broadly speaking, employers are now responsible for paying SSP to their employees during absence caused by sickness for up to eight weeks in each tax year. SSP payments received by employees are taxable and subject to National Insurance deductions in the normal way, unlike

DHSS sickness benefit. Provided employers operate the scheme properly, they may recover all SSP payments made to employees by making appropriate deductions from subsequent National Insurance or PAYE payments to the Inland Revenue.

SSP is not available to everyone at work. First, only employees may be entitled to receive payments. So the self-employed, freelancers, etc., are excluded. But certain categories of employees are also excluded. These include:

- Pensioners.
- People working under contracts of less than three months' duration.
- Those earning less than the current lower earnings limit and those 'linked' to certain state incapacity benefits.
- People on strike.
- Women during their pregnancy 'disqualifying' period.
- Those sick whilst in legal custody or abroad outside the EEC.
- Employees who have already received their maximum eight weeks' SSP entitlement during the year in question. Employees in this category should apply for DHSS sickness benefit which still remains available in the background, mainly for the longer-term sick.

Vital aspects of the SSP scheme which all small business employers must understand and act upon accordingly are:

- **Qualifying Days**   These must be agreed between the employer and each employee. They will normally (but not necessarily) reflect the employee's normal work pattern, e.g. Monday to Friday. SSP is not paid for the first three qualifying days in any period of entitlement – these are usually referred to as 'waiting days'.
- **Period of Incapacity for Work**   This is any period of four or more consecutive days of absence through illness. Periods of incapacity separated by less than 14 days are said to be 'linked' and treated as a single period, so that the employee does not have to serve his waiting days all over again.

- **Record-keeping** To ensure that the small businessman recovers all SSP payments paid out, he must keep proper records for three years after the end of the tax year to which they relate. Records in respect of each employee must cover such information as qualifying days agreed, periods of incapacity for work, amounts of SSP paid out and reasons for refusing to pay SSP.

- **Notification and Certification of Absence** Employers are allowed considerable freedom of choice in establishing their own rules for notification of absence and certification of sickness – and again, it is advisable to keep careful records. Self-certification of sickness absence is now well established. Most employers only require a doctor's note where the absence extends beyond seven days.

Finally, the wise small business operator will try to ensure that the rules of his own firm's OSP scheme (if he has one) coincide as far as possible with the SSP scheme requirements. Having two separate sets of rules applicable to the same employees causes inevitable additional administrative work for the hard-pressed and short-staffed businessman.

40

When is Notice Not Needed?

● **Are there any circumstances in which we are entitled to dismiss an employee without giving him notice or pay in lieu?**

Yes – there are four.

First, an employee is entitled to such notice as is agreed; in the absence of notice, to such period as is reasonable; and in any event, to not less than the statutory minimum, i.e. 1 week after 4 weeks' employment; 2 weeks after 2 years; and then adding a week a year up to a maximum statutory minimum of 12 weeks after 12 years.

If, then, the employee has been on your books for less than four weeks, so that there is no required statutory minimum, and if you have neither agreed to give him notice, nor is it 'reasonable' to do so, he will be entitled to none.

Second, at the other end of life's work span, if you have a normal retirement age – probably 60 for women or 65 for men – then strictly speaking there is no requirement that you give a person notice that he will have to go when he reaches that age. In practice and sometimes as a result of custom and always as a kindness, a reminder by way of notice should be given.

Third, if you employ someone on a fixed-term contract, it will expire 'by effluxion of time'. When the period runs out, so does the employee's entitlement to his money. However, where a fixed-term contract expires, the employee is 'deemed' to have been dismissed and will have his normal unfair dismissal and redundancy remedies (where applicable). *Exception:* if the fixed term is for a period of one year or more and the contract contains a 'contracting out' clause, under which the employee gives up his right to go to a tribunal.

These rules do not give the employee a right to notice when his fixed term expires, but they provide an alternative remedy which requires careful watching. That remedy does not apply, though, when the employee is taken on to do a fixed job, as opposed to being employed for a fixed time.

Finally and most important, an employee forfeits his right to notice or pay in lieu if he has done something so dreadful as to destroy the contract. If he has smashed the arrangement, then he cannot expect his employer either to give him notice or to pay him money in its place.

To amount to a 'repudiation' of the contract of service, though, the misconduct must be very serious – either one isolated act of wickedness or a number of minor misdemeanours adding up to major misbehaviour.

If in doubt about whether notice or pay in lieu need be given, then you should always pay, so as to avoid a wrongful dismissal claim. But you should state that the payment is made 'without prejudice' to your contention that the employee is not entitled to receive it by law.

41

Written Reasons for Dismissal

- **If you dismiss an employee, in what circumstances are you bound to give him written reasons for his discharge?**

While the qualifying period for unfair dismissal protection is one year (or two years in the case of small businesses), a dismissed employee is still entitled to written reasons for his dismissal after only six months' service. This will not only help him to launch an unfair dismissal claim in those rare cases where discrimination (sex, race or trade union) may be provable. But he may also be helped to show that he was dismissed 'wrongfully', i.e. without proper notice or pay in lieu. And if adequate reasons are not supplied within fourteen days of the request, he may have an independent claim for two weeks' pay.

An employer who is asked to give 'written reasons' should always do so with care. The dismissed employee is considering litigation and he will probably have been advised by a lawyer to ask for particulars. Even if the application is in the employee's own clumsy words, they may well have been drafted for him by a lawyer.

If the employer has given previous written warning to the employee, he should quote that warning in the notice and complain of non-compliance. But it has been held that mere reference to the warning is not enough. Reasons for the dismissal must still be set out in full.

The aggrieved, dismissed employee who has not received written reasons should certainly ask for them. If he receives none – or if those given are inadequate – he will be entitled to claim two weeks' pay. And it seems that a claim under this heading may be brought, even if the employee does not qualify for unfair dismissal protection.

If, on the other hand, particulars are supplied, the employer will be tied to them. He will find it difficult, if not impossible, to claim at a later stage that the reasons for the dismissal were different from those contained in the notice. Either way, the employee cannot lose by demanding written details. The employer has two weeks within which to provide them.

So while dismissed employees should make use of their power to demand written reasons, their employers should provide those particulars, with care and circumspection. They should only draft those particulars themselves if they are quite sure of their ground. Otherwise, they should take legal advice.

42
How Much Redundancy Pay?

- **If you make an employee redundant, what are his rights?**

Notice or pay in lieu

If you dismiss an employee as redundant, then he is entitled to his notice or pay in lieu on the normal basis. In addition, he gets such redundancy pay as you may agree to give him – subject to a statutory minimum.

The law, then, lays down a statutory *minimum* redundancy pay only. After two years' service after reaching the age of 18, an employee becomes entitled to a statutory payment. This increases on a sliding scale, depending upon his age, service and salary, reaching a maximum of £4,200 after 20 years.

Statutory redundancy pay

Assuming that you have the money, you will pay the full statutory redundancy entitlement and can then reclaim 41 per cent from the Redundancy Fund. If a business becomes insolvent, then the full statutory redundancy entitlement is paid out of public money.

Many employers pay more than the statutory minimum, either through kindness or to preserve the goodwill of their remaining employees or under union pressure. But they can claim no rebate on any sum over and above the minimum amount that they are required to pay by law.

Unfair dismissal claims

Apart from considering redundancy pay as such, you should consider with great care the basis for your redundancies, so as to ensure if you can that you are not faced with a series of unfair dismissal claims. If you are unfair in selecting people for redundancy, then in addition to their redundancy money they may also get compensation for unfair dismissal – all of which, of course, will be paid out of your pocket and none from public funds.

43

Damages - for Breach of Contract

- **If you dismiss an employee without proper notice, then you are breaking his contract of employment and he is entitled to damages for that breach.**

- **So how much would he get?**

- **What are the rules on damages – for breach of this or any other sort of legally binding agreement?**

Compensation

Damages for breach of contract are normally designed to compensate. Their object is to put the innocent party in the same position, financially at least, as he would have been had the contract been honoured by the other party. If you dismiss summarily, without just cause, you (on behalf of your company or firm or yourself, as the case may be) repudiate the contract of service. Hence, the business becomes liable to pay damages. Prima facie, the amount of the employee's loss is the amount of wages in lieu of notice that he should have received (see page 143 for his additional remedies for unfair dismissal, i.e. where the employer has acted unreasonably).

If the rules ended there, all would be reasonably simple. But they do not. There is a standard principle of contract law that a person who suffers as a result of a breach must do what he can to 'mitigate his damage'. He must, that is, keep it as low as he reasonably can. If you are convicted of a crime, your lawyer will make a 'plea in mitigation', begging the court to keep down the sentence. Where

139

there is a breach of contract, the sufferer must do what he can to keep his loss to a minimum.

Example 1 Suppose that your company puts in an order for goods. Delivery is not received. The company may not take no action, do nothing and sue for any loss of profit which it suffers as a result, even if the whole plant has to close down. It must seek to mitigate its loss by getting the goods elsewhere. If it has to pay more, then its 'damage' will be the difference between the price which it would have paid, had the contract been honoured, and the price which it had to pay as a result of the breach. Equally, if it manages to get the same goods at the same price, it will have suffered no loss, so no damages will be recoverable. If it manages to get in the material for an even lower price, it will have made a profit. And that will not only be a piece of good fortune for the company but also for the contract breaker.

Example 2 Or suppose that you book rooms in some splendid seaside hotel for a sales conference. For some reason the conference is called off. You have broken your contract with the hotel and you are liable to pay damages. But the hotel cannot simply leave the rooms empty and charge your company. It must do what it can to rent the rooms to others. If it fails, then you will be unlucky. If it succeeds the hotel will have mitigated its damage and have suffered no loss.

Applying the rules Now apply these rules to the employee summarily dismissed. He must seek other employment, as soon as he can. He must do his best to get another job. If he tries, but fails, then his damage will be the full amount of the wages in lieu which he should have received. If he succeeds, then any wages that he manages to earn during the period of notice together with unemployment pay received, employment expenses saved and tax and stoppages unendured will be deducted from the wages in lieu in ascertaining his damages. If he gets another job, either at the same salary and right away, or at a higher salary, he will have suffered no loss, will not be entitled to any compensation and will get no damages from the contract-breaking employers.

140

- 'If I dismiss without justification, can I pay wages in lieu of compensation right away?' You can.

- 'But if I wait until after the period of notice has expired, there's an excellent chance that the person will get less?' There is.

- 'If he has managed to get some other work, the wages received will be deductible from the wages in lieu – so we may have to pay little or nothing?' Correct.

- 'And if he got no further work, we'll only have to pay him the lot if he can show that he did not relax and have a holiday at our expense – that he really tried to get back into harness?' Yes. If you want to be nasty, you may dismiss summarily when you have no just cause for doing so, and then sit back and hope for the best. You will probably save your company some money. Equally, you are unlikely to contribute to good industrial relations. And if the dismissal was 'unfair', watch out for trouble from the tribunals.

44

Constructive Dismissal

- Is it true that an employee who resigns his job and accepts money in full and final settlement of his claim against the company may still go to an industrial tribunal and claim that he was dismissed unfairly?

What is constructive dismissal?

If you force an employee into resigning, then he is said to be dismissed 'constructively'. If you have made it impossible for him to stay on . . . turn him out of his job . . . or, as an Appeal Court recently put it, if you have 'squeezed him out', then you have destroyed his contract and he can claim that he was sacked. You have given him no alternative and therefore though physically he has left, you have terminated the agreement.

The law normally prevents an employee from contracting out of his right to go to an industrial tribunal, to claim either an unfair dismissal or a redundancy remedy. So the settlement you have made with him will not generally be binding upon him – unless it has been recorded by a Conciliation Officer.

Recording a settlement

If, then, you had known enough to call in an ACAS official and he had made a note of the settlement, on his form COT3, then it would have been binding. **As it is, no ACAS record means no effective agreement**. Your employee may go to the tribunal, claim that he was dismissed 'constructively' and if the tribunal agrees with him, then he may claim that his sacking was unfair. If it was, then he will be entitled to a compensatory award, to cover his lost pay – up to a maximum of £7,500; to a basic award – his lost statutory redundancy entitlement – which, after 20 years could be as high as £4,200; and if you are ordered to take him back and you unreasonably refuse, then he could get an 'additional award' – although in practice, this rarely happens.

So next time: if you make a settlement with a departing employee, call in the ACAS man to record it.

45

Sacking Suspects

- **Can you sack an employee if you suspect him of stealing?**
- **If you catch him red-handed, can you do a deal with him?**

Sacking on suspicion

The remarkable decision in the case involving employees of the Coral Leisure Group showed the strength of the employer when dealing with suspects. Do what is 'reasonable' and whether or not your suspicion is justified, the employee will almost certainly be dismissed 'fairly'.

Briefly, two men held the key to a safe. Money was missing. But which one of the two was the thief – or did both of them combine? Without any evidence as to which of the two was guilty, Corals sacked both. One of them brought a claim to an industrial tribunal, claiming that the dismissal was unfair.

The employers admitted that they had not one shred of evidence to show that the claimant was the guilty party. But, they maintained, they had a 'substantial reason' for the dismissal. And they acted 'reasonably' in treating that reason as sufficient to warrant depriving the employee of his livelihood.

An Appeal Court agreed. What would a reasonable, average, sensible employer have done? Would he have kept both on when no evidence was available? Or would he have placed the key to that small part of his fortune safely in the hands of other people?

Unanimously, the Judges decided that an employer, acting reasonably, would have done the same as Corals. As they could not decide between the two alternative suspects, they really had no alternative other than to sack both – which they had done.

The moral from this sad tale: You do not have to wait until the employee is prosecuted nor, still less, until he is convicted when deciding whether or not to terminate his employment. You are not sacking him because he is a convicted thief.

Caught red-handed

Suppose that you catch an employee stealing. You are not bound to hand him over to justice. You may, if you wish, turf him out. You may even do a deal and say that in return for his giving you back what he has taken, you will not inform the authorities.

If you do decide to hand the suspect over to justice, the police will prosecute if – but only if – they wish. If the employee then pleads 'Not guilty' it may be many months before he comes up for trial, especially if he elects to be tried by jury at a Crown Court.

Meanwhile, what are you to do? The employee is presumed innocent of any crime until he is found guilty. But are you to suspend him on full pay until that decision is made? The law – and successive cases – give the clear answer: No. If you dismiss the man, you do so not because of any conviction, but because he has behaved in such a way that a reasonable employer would not keep him on.

Suspicions   Maybe the employee had your equipment or stock in his home . . . someone else's handbag or wallet in his possession. . . . Then you are dismissing him because of his suspicious behaviour. He will only be convicted of theft if the prosecution can prove 'beyond all reasonable doubt' that he intended 'permanently to deprive' the owner of his goods. You are dismissing him because he was in breach of your rules . . . because the suspicion resting upon him was so heavy that you could not reasonably be expected to keep him at work . . . or even, perhaps, because other employees were not prepared to work with him.

An unfair dismissal claim?   Naturally, if you do dismiss in that way, you are taking a chance. If the employee does bring an unfair dismissal claim against you, then it will cost you money – win or lose. If the case reaches trial, you will probably win – about 72 per cent of unfair dismissal claims fail. But the cost of winning may stretch into thousands of pounds.

If, then, you decide to pay off the suspect, you may save money. But equally, once you have made him a payment, you may have difficulty in showing that you regarded his conduct as really serious.

The answer, in practice, is simple. Make the payment 'without prejudice'. Write something like this:

❝ While in our view as a result of your conduct, we would be entitled to dismiss you summarily, we have no wish to cause additional hardship to your family . . . you have been with the company for many years . . . and in the circumstances, we are paying you your money in lieu of notice, but *without prejudice* to our contention that you could be dismissed summarily. ❞

If you come to some agreement with the suspect, then you must have that agreement recorded by a Conciliation Officer, otherwise it will not be binding. Remember: fixed-term contracts apart, an employee can only successfully contract out of his right to take his claim to an industrial tribunal, if that agreement is recorded by an ACAS man on his form COT3.

Offences away from work

What difference does it make, then, if the employee's suspicious behaviour occurred outside work? Here the ACAS Code gives guidance. You may not automatically dismiss an employee who is arrested for an alleged offence outside work, but you may dismiss him if his conduct made it impossible for him properly to do his job. A driver who loses his licence can scarcely save his position by saying:

❝ I lost it through driving dangerously in my own time! ❞

Also, there are offences committed outside work which make the employee unacceptable to his colleagues. These usually involve sex offences against children.

So if you do suspect an employee of stealing or of some other offence, assess the evidence; follow a fair procedure; listen to his explanation, however unlikely; give him the right to appeal to a higher level of authority, if you have one – and then make up your mind. Corals' case showed that you are likely to be much stronger in dealing with suspects than most recruiters realized.

46

References

- **Is anyone bound to give a reference?**

- **What can the employee do if his former employers refuse to do so – or worse, if they speak ill of him?**

- **As an employer, are you in trouble if your ex-employee discovers that you have given him a bad reference – or if, through some careless mistake, you mislead the recipient?**

Disclaimers

The case of *Hedley Byrne & Company Limited* v. *Heller & Partners Limited* reached the House of Lords. The plaintiffs wanted a reference for a company. The defendants' bankers obliged. They said, in effect, that the company was worthy of the confidence which the plaintiffs proposed to place in it. In reliance on the reference, the plaintiffs proceeded to give credit of over £17,000 to the company – which promptly went into liquidation and the £17,000 disappeared forever. So Hedley Byrne sued Heller & Partners, claiming damages on the ground that the reference was given 'negligently'. The bank had a duty to 'exercise care in giving the reference', said the plaintiffs. 'They were careless. We lost our money. We are entitled to get it back from them.'

'Nonsense', the bank retorted. 'We gave the reference as a matter of courtesy. We were not negligent. And anyway, the reference carried a disclaimer. It read: "For your private use and without responsibility on the part of the bank or its officials".'

The trial judge decided that there had been negligence but that as the free information was given 'without responsibility', the claim failed. The House of Lords held that the disclaimer was sufficient to let the bank off the hook. Lord Reid said that

❝ a reasonable man, knowing that he was being trusted or that his skill and judgement were being relied on, would, I think, have three courses open to him. He could keep silent or decline to give the information or advice sought; or he could give an answer with a clear qualification that he accepted no responsibility for it or that it was given without the reflection or the enquiry which a careful answer would require; or he could simply answer without such qualification. If he chooses to adopt the last course he must, I think, be held to have accepted some responsibility for his answer being given carefully. . . . **❞**

If you are asked for a reference, then, you are free to decline. You are not bound to bestow on others the benefit of your gratuitous advice.

If you are asked for a reference and you give a reference, you (like the bank) are fully entitled to say:

❝ All right. Here are my views. But you take them at your own risk. **❞**

If you simply give a reference, without a disclaimer, then – even though you are doing a favour to another businessman – you are bound to take reasonable care to ensure that the statement you make is correct, provided that the advice was given in the ordinary course of your business. Free advice may prove very expensive – not only to the recipient but also to the kindly donor.

Unfavourable references

What of the employee who is dissatisfied with his reference? He was not entitled to insist upon getting one in the first place. If it turns out that he would have been better off without one, he will rarely have any redress.

Now suppose that the reference is unfavourable. You have 'defamed' the person named. If the reference was given in writing, it is libellous; if oral, it is a slander. In either event, you risk being sued. But the risk is minute.

The law realizes that it is essential that business people give references. So it says: 'The occasion upon which a reference is given is privileged'. The giver has a moral duty to supply the

149

information and the prospective employer (or creditor, as in Hedley Byrne's case) a direct interest in receiving it. So a successful action in defamation will only lie if there is 'malice' – which, in law, means some unlawful motive – generally, a desire to harm the person named, rather than the wish to assist another employer who asks for the reference.

There are other almost insurmountable legal and practical obstacles for the unfortunate person defamed in a reference. For instance: how will he prove what has been said? And can he afford to pay for his case, as no legal aid is available for defamation actions and he is almost certainly out of a job?

If you are asked for a reference and wish to be frank, tell the relevant prospective employer to speak to you by telephone. What you say may be just as defamatory as if you had written it, but if the employee wants to take action against you, he will have much greater difficulty in proving his case. Conversely, if you want a frank reference, experience (rather than law) indicates that you should ask for it by word of mouth. You are more likely to get the answer you need.

If you want a reference for yourself, apply these rules in reverse. You will find yourself very much in the hands of your ex-employers. The law is on their side – if they only know it.

In practice, defamation actions arising out of unfavourable references are almost unknown. So here is a summary of the rules:

- Instruct your manager to add a footnote to every reference given: 'While we are pleased to provide references for ex-employees/customers/clients, all references are given without legal responsibility'. This will free all concerned from any liability arising under the Hedley Byrne principle.
- Avoid malice in references – but do not waste energy on possible defamation actions arising through unsatisfactory references – the chances of litigation are highly remote.
- If you yourself cannot get a reference – or a decent reference – from former employers, waste no time, in energy or cash, in pursuit of legal remedy. Instead, tell prospective employers

the truth. Thus: 'My best reference – my years of service –
and the way I was promoted. I only left because of ill-will
which was in no way of my making – but which, of course,
inevitably means that you will not get a fair reference from
them. . . .'

47

Unlawful Competition

- **If your neighbours start supplying goods or services in competition to you, what can you do about it – apart from protesting to them?**

Meeting competition

Unfortunately, the odds are that you will either have to put up with your neighbour's competition or meet it in your own way. There is no law to prevent them from going into your line. So if they insist upon undermining your business, you might try doing the same to theirs – like selling some of the items which they carry in stock. When they see that two can play at the same game, they may be prepared to be neighbourly and sensible.

There is, though, just one legal hope for you. If you and your neighbours are in the same set of buildings, you may have the same landlords. There may then be a term in the lease of each of you, confining you to your particular trade. These 'mutual covenants' are designed to protect each trader against unfair competition from the other. If they exist, then you should at once prod your landlord and try to get him to lean on your neighbours.

So if you are a tenant, check your lease. If you find a restrictive covenant which limits your rights to sell, your neighbour may well have the same problem with his own. In that case, you should get your mutual landlords on the trail without delay. And if in doubt, consult your solicitor.

48

Short-time Working

- **When are you entitled to put employees on to short-time working if trade is slow?**

If your employees have a guaranteed working week, then you cannot cut it down without their consent. But if times are sufficiently bad and your employees see that redundancies would be the alternative to agreement, you may well get their consent. With unemployment so high and jobs so hard to get, most people who are put on to short time accept the position – however reluctantly.

If you keep people on short time for long enough, though, then they may apply to you to be restored to full time and if you fail to do so, then they may regard themselves as dismissed as redundant. The rules are complicated and if you run into this sort of misery, you should put all the facts before your lawyer and get his help in planning your tactics.

49

Time Off Work – the Latest Rules

- **When is an employee entitled as of right to time off work – with or without pay?**

- **How are the statutory rights, as explained by the Time Off Work Code, working in practice?**

- **And how are these affected by recent legislation?**

Any employee remains entitled to such time off work as may be reasonable in all the circumstances of the case:

- For public duties – such as those of a JP, school governor, local councillor or member of a statutory authority. An employer is not required by law to pay the employee when he is off work for this reason.

- When the employee is made redundant, he is entitled to reasonable time off work at his normal pay in order to seek *(a)* alternative work and /or *(b)* training for such work.

- A trade union official may claim paid time off work for trade union duties. These include not only duties in connection with collective bargaining but those 'concerned with industrial relations with his employer or any associated employer or employee' – plus training for such duties.

- An expectant mother is now (thanks to the *Employment Act 1980*) entitled to reasonable time off work without loss of normal pay, to attend upon a doctor or midwife for ante-natal advice and care. If required by her employer, she must produce a certificate of pregnancy and (after the first occasion) evidence of her appointment.

- A safety representative is entitled to reasonable time off work for the carrying out of his duties (as laid down by the Health and Safety Regulations, Code and Guidance on Safety Representatives and Committees).

ACAS Time Off Work Code

The ACAS Time Off Work Code expands the rules as they apply to trade union officials and members. The Code also suggests that it may be in the interests of management as well as of unions that election meetings and those concerned with possible industrial action should be well attended. In practice, management almost always recognizes that it is in their interests to achieve a maximum attendance. Election meetings (and sometimes others) are now more often than not held in working hours and without loss of pay, by members as well as by officials. This remarkable evolution is having and will continue to have far more effect upon union meetings than the 1980 Act provisions entitling unions to claim the cost of secret ballots from public funds.

50

The Legal Effect of Codes

- What is the effect of a 'Code of Practice'?

- If your driver is in breach of the Highway Code, what could happen to him?

It is neither a civil nor a criminal offence to be in breach of a Code of Practice. But any failure to comply with its terms may be used in evidence against you in any proceedings to which they are relevant.

So your driver will not be prosecuted for breach of the Highway Code but if he is 'done' for, say, 'careless driving' and it can be shown that he was in breach of the Code, his conviction becomes far more likely.

In the same way, you should comply with the ACAS Disciplinary Code. This provides (among other requirements) that you give at least one written warning of intended dismissal, where reasonably practicable. Failure to do so is not an offence. But if the unwarned employee takes you to an industrial tribunal, claiming that his dismissal was 'unfair', your prospects of losing are increased. Conversely, if you comply with the Code and follow a recommended procedure you will probably win. Indeed, with luck you may avoid the trouble altogether. The claimant may be advised that his case is hopeless.

51

A Right to Organize

- Unions rarely bother to organize staff in small businesses but the larger yours grows – or the greater the number of branches in your chain – the more likely you are to need to know if a union organizer is entitled to come into your business to talk to your staff or to hold a meeting?

- Does a union have the right to organize?

You are not entitled to 'discriminate' against an employee in selection, promotion, transfer, training or dismissal because he wishes to belong to or to take part in the activities of an independent trade union. But you are under no legal obligation to provide facilities for a trade union organization.

Refusing access

The organizer may only enter your premises with your permission, express or implied. If he comes in unauthorized, then he is a 'trespasser'. You may ask him to leave and if he refuses, you may (at least in theory) use reasonable force to eject him. And you could, if necessary, claim an injunction – an order of the court, restraining him from coming on to your premises without your consent.

That said, is it really intelligent to refuse access to the union official? Or will that lead to ill will and even propel people into joining, whereas otherwise they might have preferred to stay out? Do you really think that hostility to unions and their officers leads to good industrial relations? And what makes you think that in the long run your employees will not join unions – unless they feel that

157

they are getting at least as good conditions by remaining outside a union as they would if they joined?

Anyway, the law allows you to exclude union organizers – but not to discriminate against its potential or would-be members. The rest is a matter for your own decision.

52

Industrial Tribunals and Costs

- **If you are involved in industrial tribunal proceedings, what are your chances of getting an award of costs against the applicant if his claim fails?**

Tribunals now have power to award costs where a claim is brought or pursued 'frivolously' or 'vexatiously' or (this is new, since the 1980 Industrial Tribunal Regulations) 'unreasonably'. In theory, then, tribunals now have a very wide discretion.

Awards

In practice, though, awards of costs are seldom made against unsuccessful claimants and when they are, the amount is likely to be somewhere between £50 and £100. As it generally costs an employer between £600 and £6,000 to win a tribunal case, the costs awarded tend to be insignificant. So if you do fight the case, you must reckon that you will have to pay for it.

Pre-hearing assessment

If the claim is so entirely without merit, you might consider asking the tribunal for a 'pre-hearing assessment'. This feature (initiated under the 1980 Regulations) is intended to operate as a sieve, to get rid of hopeless cases like that of your employee. It operates with fluctuating success in various parts of the country. Have a word with your solicitor and see whether he would recommend sparking it off in your case. Failure with the pre-hearing assessment may add to your costs and encourage your former employee to put a much higher value on his claim if you want to settle it than might be the case otherwise.

On the other hand, if the tribunal does indicate to the employee that the case is not worth pursuing, then it might disappear at this stage. Alternatively, your prospect of getting costs from the employee if he does persist and lose as expected will improve.

53

Trade Unions and 'Recognition'

- **If employees ask you to 'recognize' and to bargain with their trade union, are you bound to agree?**
- **What does 'recognition' mean in practice?**

A trade union is a workers' organization. Its job is to look after the interests of its members.

In general, the only unions that are given rights are those that are certified by the Certification Officer as 'independent' of managerial control. And only those that are 'recognized' to any substantial extent for the purposes of collective bargaining are entitled to insist:

- That you bargain with them.
- That you disclose information about your business, necessary to them for that bargaining.
- That you give them advance notice of proposed redundancies.
- That you accept their appointed safety representatives.
- That you respect the protection which the law gives them and their officials against civil and criminal suits, when they act 'in contemplation or furtherance of a trade dispute'.

So if the union is 'recognized', its representatives will bargain with you about the terms and conditions of work of its members. Almost inevitably, any agreement that you make with the union will be reflected in the terms of other non-members. You will be switching from individual to collective bargaining. In the process, your hand will probably be weakened and the position of the employees strengthened. After all, individually they have little 'clout', while together they may have considerable strength.

You will probably not agree to recognize a union unless it includes a majority of your employees in the particular category among its membership. But there is no rule or limit laid down by law.

If you cannot come to an agreement with the union, you may bring in the ACAS Conciliation Officer to seek his advice or even, with the agreement of the union, its intervention. But the *Employment Act 1980* repealed the recognition procedures. So recognition disputes have to be sorted out through shop floor bargaining and muscle.

54

Temporary, Part-time, Seasonal and Agency Workers

- **What are the legal rights of non-permanent employees?**

- **When are they protected and against what – and by whom?**

- **If you recruit non-permanent or non-full-time workers, what precautions should you take – for their protection and for yours?**

- **If you have to dismiss them, then what are the legal rules?**

- **What is the difference between a 'fixed term' and a 'fixed job' employee?**

- **And what about agency employees – how do they fit into the legal picture?**

Here, then, is a summary and survey of the rules – as every small businessman needs to know them.

An 'employee' is a person who serves under a contract of employment. He is 'temporary' if his job is not permanent. And he is 'part-time' if his work is not full-time. So much for the dictionary – now for the law!

Protection of 'temps'

An employee is protected by the law once he has been 'continuously employed' for at least one year – or two years in the

163

case of businesses with less than 20 employees. When the qualifying period for protection was 26 weeks, many 'seasonal' employees had exactly the same protection as 'permanents'. But now, very few 'temporary' appointments last long enough for the employment protection rules to apply.

Many 'temps' though are agency employees. Then their protection lies against their employers – the agency concerned – and not against the outfit for whom they are actually working. If you take on an agency 'temp', then he (or she) will have exactly the same rights against the agency as your own employees enjoy against you.

If you take on agency staff, then they will almost always cost you more than equivalent workers on your own payroll. But you are partially buying freedom from the protection which your own staff could wield against you. The agency's rights and responsibilities and your own will depend largely upon the contract between you. The employee is on hire – even if in practice he remains for ever.

Naturally, you may come to some arrangement with the agency to acquire the permanent services of the 'temp', as your employee. In that case, the period of continuous employment will date from the day when he began working for you as your employee, and not when he physically began carrying out work for you or on your behalf.

Part-timers

In law, a 'part-timer' is a person who normally works less than 16 hours a week – or 8 hours after 5 years' continuous service. Once he exceeds these hours, he has exactly the rights of any full-timer, including protection against unfair dismissal, the right to written particulars of his main terms of service within three months of the start of the employment or four weeks from any change, redundancy rights and (in the case of women) maternity pay and leave.

Remember, the hours which count are those which the employee is entitled to work. Overtime, which is in the employer's discretion, is not included, even if it is regularly worked.

Suppose, then, that you take on an employee and do not know how much work will be available for him and for how long. You have no

164

worries for nearly a year. Provided that you do not dismiss the employee on grounds of sex, race or trade union discrimination, you may 'get rid' of any employee, as unfairly as you like, with no interference from the law. Morality and good management apart, your main trouble will arise if the employee is protected by a trade union. Employees have their main rights by agreement; the law provides statutory minimum entitlements in some cases; but the job of a union is to ensure in so far as it can that its member is treated fairly and gets the best terms and conditions available.

Trial periods

It follows that even with temporary employees, trial or probationary periods are normally out of date and useless. What is the point of telling an employee: 'We're watching you', if you already have what amounts to a twelve-month statutory trial period during which, subject to union pressure, you have the sole decision on dismissal, without fear of legal intrusion.

Anyway, if you provide a trial period – to give yourself the theoretical option of making temporary what may be permanent employment – you may provide exactly the opposite of that which you intend. If, for instance, you say to a newcomer: 'I'll give you a three-month trial' and you then decide to dismiss him after a week, he will probably be entitled to the rest of his three months' pay. You could, of course, have said: 'For the first three months, your employment will be subject to one week's notice on either side' – but you did not.

Temporary and fixed-term appointments

To avoid trouble with an employee who you may not be able to keep on at the end of a job, a transaction or a foreseeable period, your should make it clear that the employment is offered only on that basis. If an employee accepts a job knowing that it is for a fixed purpose, then you do not even need to include a 'contracting-out clause' in his agreement. The law will achieve that result for you. Indeed, a recent appeal decision made a clear distinction between a 'fixed-job' and a 'fixed-term' contract.

Suppose that you take on an employee to accomplish a particular task, alone or with others. He is employed by you; his continuous employment normally begins on his first day of work; and if you do not keep him on when the job is finished, then (says the law) you are not 'dismissing' him at all. You are not terminating his contract. It comes automatically to an end, along with the job for which he was employed.

Now suppose that you take on an employee for a fixed term – fixed for 12 or 18 or 24 months, for example. You are giving him the certainty of employment and if the fixed term is for 12 months or more, then you may include an effective clause in the contract under which the employee agrees not to seek unfair dismissal or redundancy rights if he is not kept on when the period expires.

The *Employment Protection (Consolidation) Act 1978* specifically provides that where a fixed-term contract expires and the employee is not kept on by the employer, then he is deemed to have been 'dismissed'. He will then have the same unfair dismissal rights as he would if he had been sacked 'actually' or 'constructively'.

Normally, the law does not allow an employee to 'contract out' of his right to go to a tribunal. There are two exceptions to the rule:

- An agreement to compromise a claim will be binding on the employee if – but only if – it is recorded by a Conciliation Officer. The ACAS man has no right to approve or to disapprove of the settlement, but only to record it on his form COT3.
- A contracting-out clause in a fixed-term contract of 12 months or more will be effective. So if you are giving an employee that sort of security of tenure, then you may deprive him of the additional protection of unfair dismissal and redundancy – assuming, of course, that he is prepared to enter your service on that basis.

However, there is no point in including a similar clause in a 'fixed job' contract. You do not need it because the employee is not deemed to have been dismissed if you do not keep him in your service when the job is done.

Seasonal workers

Some unscrupulous employers try to keep the weight of the law off their backs by making permanent staff into temporary staff. This can in theory be achieved by breaking the continuity of employment before the employees achieve the protection of the law. If you take on employees on a seasonal basis and lay them off between seasons, then they will never achieve the protection which continuity gives them. If you provide a retainer so as to keep the employee attached to you, knowing that you will want him back when your season of activity returns, then you may be creating a continuity. After all, you cannot both keep the person as your employee while at the same time cutting him clear from continuity. If in doubt, you should consult your lawyer.

If, though, the employee remains with you from year to year, you cannot deprive him of his rights by making a false and fraudulent break in the employment. The law lays down no period during which the employee must be away from you, if he is to lose his rights. Looking at the 'reality and not at the form', the question would be: 'Was the break genuine? Or was the employment continuous?' I repeat: if in doubt, check with your legal adviser.

Nowadays, fixed-term contracts usually apply to apprentices, to some top-level executives and to some academic and entertainment posts. Fixed-job contracts range from consultancies to work of maintenance and repair.

The rights of the temporary worker

Now assume that an employee is genuinely 'temporary'. What rights does he enjoy in law – and what additional protection should you give him?

Even a temporary employee works under a 'contract of employment'. His rights depend upon his agreement with you. He will be entitled, for instance, to his contractual notice or pay in lieu, to his remuneration and fringe benefits and to those privileges contained in his contract. Conversely, he will be subject to the disciplinary, grievance and other procedures expressly or implicitly included in his terms of service.

Written terms   Once the employee is with you for more than 13 weeks and assuming that he is not a part-timer (as defined), he is entitled to his main terms of service in writing. My advice: you should provide them even for those who work for you for shorter periods. After all, the purpose of writing is to avoid disputes. And even an employee who cannot take his dispute to an industrial tribunal may cause trouble, union or no union. And anyway, even if the law does not require the provision of terms, good management certainly does.

If a temporary employee is killed while working for you and you were at fault, it will not provide you with any defence to say: 'Well – she was only a temp!' An employee's tenure on life is not limited by the temporary nature of his or her employment.

So you must apply the rules on health and safety at work for the benefit of your temporary employees, in exactly the same way as you do for those who are permanent. Section 2 of the Health and Safety at Work Act applies to all employees. But conversely, a temporary employee is under the same duty to take care for his own safety and for that of fellow employees as is anyone permanently on your payroll.

Finally, note that part-timers are entitled to sick pay under the SSP scheme (see page 130) provided that they earn more than the current lower earnings limit. The only temporary workers who are excluded from SSP are those whose contract of service is for a specified period of three months or less.

So try to decide when you take on an employee whether the job is to be temporary or permanent. If there is doubt, say so. Put the main terms clearly on to paper and make sure that your employee understands his rights and his obligations – and the limits on yours. Avoid misunderstanding and you will keep a decent and inexpensive distance from the law. But ignore the rules – or fall out with unions over the rights of their members, temporary or permanent – and bad management will supplement your failure to comply with the law and ensure that you are involved in trouble which would otherwise be so easily avoidable.

55

Your Rights Against Your Own Company

- **You run a small business through your own family company. You own the majority of the shares and your wife and children the balance.**

- **What are the rights of each of you against the company?**

- **Are you 'employees' even though you own the business.**

Separate legal entities

A company is a 'separate legal entity' from those who own the shares. That is why a shareholder is rarely personally liable for a company's debts.

It follows that if you are employed by a company, you have the same rights against that company as any other employee.

Unfortunately, members of families sometimes fall out. Husbands and wives divorce or children quarrel. If a member of the family is employed by the company, he has (in theory – and sometimes in practice) the same rights against the employing company as he would have if its shares were owned by total strangers.

Too many small businesses ignore these rules and do not even bother to set out the rights of family employees. Disputes apart, if the company is sold or merged or taken over, the absence of properly recorded rights often leads to unnecessary trouble and weakens the bargaining position of the family employees.

The remedy, of course, lies in the shareholders' hands. They should get sensible terms of service drawn up by their solicitors, before problems arise.

56
Acquisitions

- **You operate a small but successful business and have decided to expand.**

- **The owners of a small local competitor have offered to sell you their business at what you regard as a bargain price.**

Assessing the value

First, check out your bargain and make sure that it is worth acquiring. Get your accountants on the trail to examine their books. And check their assets to make sure that you acquire the maximum; and check their liabilities, so as to decide the best way to make your acquisition.

For instance, suppose that the other business is being run through a company. You could simply buy the shares. But the company would continue in business as before. Or the company could go into liquidation and you could bid for the assets.

Once you know (for example) the real as opposed to the book value of the assets as well as the reality of the liabilities, you should then discuss the best method of acquisition with your solicitor. He will also guide you with other complications, including the problems of dismissing or taking over employees. These altered thanks to regulations on the Transfer of Undertakings which (in broad terms) preserve continuity of employment for people who get taken over along with a business and (in theory, although rarely in practice) make it more difficult to dismiss employees acquired as a result of the transfer, merger or acquisition.

You will also need help in connection with the conveyance of premises or other property. Under no circumstances should you enter into any agreement for acquisition without guidance from both your solicitor and your accountant.

Section 6

Negligence, Occupiers' Liability and Health and Safety

57

The Health and Safety at Work Act

- **What are the rules laid down by this Act?**
- **How do they affect the small business?**

The law on an employee's safety at work comes under two main headings – criminal and civil. The object of the criminal law is to impose standards for the protection of the community as a whole and employee safety is mainly covered by the Health and Safety at Work Act – as well as (where appropriate) by the Factories Act and by the Offices, Shops and Railway Premises Act. The civil law gives individuals rights against each other. It has arisen mainly through judges' decisions, i.e. by common law, or through the Occupiers' Liability Act.

So let's start with crime: the rules laid down by the 1974 Act and how they affect the small business.

Criminal law

The *Health and Safety at Work etc. Act 1974* has two main objects:

- To secure the health, safety and welfare of people at work.
- To protect people other than people at work against risks to health or safety arising out of or in connection with the activities of people at work.

The Act is designed to protect not only your own employees, but also contractors, sub-contractors, visitors and the general public 'affected by your undertaking'.

A general duty is imposed on an employer 'to ensure so far as is reasonably practicable, the health, safety and welfare at work of all his employees'. In place of the accumulation of responsibilities, built up through centuries of High Court decisions, the Act specifies the duty under five heads:

- The provision and maintenance of safe and satisfactory plant and 'systems of work'.
- Safety and the absence of risks to health in connection with 'the use, storage, handling and transport of articles and substances'.
- The provision of all necessary 'instruction, training and supervision'.
- The maintenance in a safe and satisfactory condition of the place of work, as well as 'means of access to and egress from it'.
- The provision and maintenance of a safe and satisfactory 'working environment', together with proper 'facilities'.

Employers must provide and bring to the notice of their employees written statements of their general policy with respect to health and safety at work and especially as to 'the organizations and arrangements for the time being in force for carrying out that policy'.

Section 3 says:

It shall be the duty of every employer to conduct his undertaking in such a way as to ensure, so far as is reasonably practicable, that persons not in his employment who may be affected thereby are not exposed to risks to their health and safety.

Combine this with Section 4 and the object becomes clear. Those who 'have control of any place where the public may use any plant or substance' must take all reasonably practicable steps to see that the public are kept safe and 'without risk to their health'.

174

Section 5 imposes a duty on any person who 'designs, manufactures, imports or supplies any article for use at work'. He must take all reasonably practicable steps, for testing, examination or otherwise, to see that such article will not cause injury to those who use it.

The employee himself has two specific statutory duties under the Act:

- To take reasonable care for the health and safety of himself and other people who may be affected by his acts or omissions at work.
- 'To co-operate' with his employer or others 'so far as is necessary' to see that statutory duties are 'performed or complied with'. But employers are not permitted to 'levy any charge' on employees in respect of anything 'done or provided in pursuance of any requirement of the relevant statutory provisions'. It may be that employees will have to be provided with any relevant safety clothing, at no charge to themselves.

So here is a code of health and safety replacing the previous hodge-podge of statutory and common law rules. To administer it there are two bodies – the Health and Safety Commission and the Health and Safety Executive.

Section 32 provides the penalties. Anyone who fails to discharge his duties or contravenes the Act or health and safety regulations or who obstructs inspectors in the course of their duties may (in most cases) now be fined by a Magistrates' Court up to £1,000 or, if convicted in a Crown Court, be fined an unlimited amount – and/or in the case of individuals, in certain cases, they may be imprisoned for up to two years.

Personal liability As usual where there are statutory offences, there are also specific defences. Anyone charged under the Act may prove that the offence was committed 'due to the act or default of some other person', and in that case 'the other person' may be charged and (if he was indeed at fault) convicted.

175

Where any offence is 'proved to have been committed with the consent or connivance of, or to have been attributable to any neglect on the part of, any director, manager, secretary or other similar officer' of a company, or of anyone 'purporting to act in any such capacity', he as well as the company, shall be guilty of the offence and liable to be punished accordingly.

It is this personal liability resting on everyone from chairman to foreman which makes the Act so formidable. If you are charged and your defence is that you took all such steps as were 'reasonably practicable' to avoid breaking the law, then the Act says that the burden of establishing your innocence rests on you. 'It shall be for the accused to prove' that the dangerous practice which the prosecution has established did not result from any default on his part.

Civil law

The same wrongful act or omission which created a statutory liability may also give rise to a civil claim for damages. If an employee is injured as a result of the breach of statutory duty, then he may be able to claim damages in a civil court.

The civil claim, though, need not be limited to a 'cause of action' founded on breach of statutes. There may be 'common law negligence'; failure to take reasonable care not to submit the employee to unnecessary risk. An employer must provide a safe system of working, reasonably competent fellow employees, adequate supervision and training and proper plant and materials and appliances – irrespective of any statute.

Employees must still take reasonable care for their own safety. Where an accident is wholly or partly caused by the employee's own failure to take reasonable care for himself, his damages are reduced in direct proportion to his own responsibility for his own downfall. Under the Act, not only must he take proper care for himself, and for other employees, but he must co-operate as necessary, so as to ensure that the law is not broken.

What of the general public? First, they have protection in cases in which previously the common law applied. Secondly, the Occupiers' Liability Act remains in force, dealing with most potential claims by members of the public. It applies to clients or customers and other welcome visitors, along with tax collectors, meter readers and others whom you would prefer to keep away. It imposes a 'common duty of care' on all occupiers, for the protection of all lawful visitors.

The Occupiers' Liability Act is a civil statute. The 1974 Act introduced criminal liability even where no accident has occurred – a liability which supplements the civil law, but does not replace it.

Finally, Regulations, Code and full Guidance Notes have laid down rules for consultation with safety representatives and for the setting up of safety committees. These rarely apply to the small business – but if you recognize a trade union for the purposes of collective bargaining, you should consult your Factory Inspector or perhaps read my *Employer's Guide to the Law on Health and Safety at Work*, so as to get the information which you will need to comply with this branch of the law.

58

Health and Safety Checklist

- **What are the main health and safety problems for the small business?**

- **Here is a checklist of twelve areas of concern**

Contracts of employment

What changes should you make in your employees' contracts of employment so as to take the Act into account? Consider especially the following:

- Should you include terms that the employee will submit to medical examinations at the request of the management? Their refusal to accept this term will cast inevitable suspicion on the person's health.

- A requirement that the employee will wear protective clothing and/or make full use of all guards or other equipment provided for his safety.

- A requirement that the employee will co-operate in all safety procedures.

Your contracts may provide that failure to comply with these rules may result in dismissal. The employee will then at least know where he stands and be unable to allege that you have sprung a legal surprise upon him.

Medical examinations

Do you arrange medical examinations for existing employees or for prospective employees? If so, are you satisfied that these are sufficient? Have you made adequate arrangements for consultant doctors – with job specifications for them to include the requirement that they supervise your compliance with your duties under the Act. They should equip themselves with the rules; make any necessary inspections within your premises or concerning your processes; and while protecting your employees against danger to their health or safety, at the same time protect you against prosecution.

Employees and safety measures

Do you operate a sufficiently firm and safe procedure to deal with employees who fail or refuse to attempt to make use of safety clothing, equipment or procedures? You must plan methods; establish procedures; insist that these be followed with as much firmness as those established in accordance with the Code of Industrial Relations for dismissal purposes; and you must decide whether and when to dismiss employees who refuse to take sufficient care for the safety of themselves or for that of their colleagues.

Bomb warnings

The commercial concern which does not suffer from 'bomb scares' is extremely fortunate. You will already have (and hopefully keep well oiled) procedures to deal with fires or fire alarms. Similar procedures are essential for bomb scares.

Consult your local police; if co-operation from authorities is inadequate, either in connection with advice or search, then consider seeking pressures from your trade association or Chamber of Commerce. Also: are you satisfied that your security arrangements are sufficient to deter would-be bombers? And have you arranged for your mail to be scanned, when letter bomb outrages are in vogue?

Insurance

Most insurance policies contain exclusion clauses. Check your policies with care, to ensure that you will remain insured, in spite of the Act. If there are exclusions in respect, for example, of breaches of the Act or damage caused by bombs, then you may have to pay an additional premium in order to exclude the exclusions. If in doubt, consult your insurance brokers or your insurers.

Written statements

The Act requires all employers to prepare and, where necessary, revise written statements of the arrangements they make for the safety and health of their employees. The statements must be brought to the notice of all employees.

Do you give a statement to all employees, separately or as part of your works or organizational rules? If so, then you may be left with the problem of providing detailed instructions for each process or job. These require careful preparation and may need checking with the factory inspector. Watch out, too, for any Codes of Practice affecting the written statement.

Documentation

Breaches of the Act may prove extremely serious. It is, therefore, vital for you to prepare your defences in advance. This may best be done by a careful system of documentation. The object of the documents: to show that your safety, health and welfare arrangements are in accordance with the Act and any default is that of 'some other person' and is not your fault.

Management at every level must be prepared to prove that they prepared and passed on adequate instructions to the next level down. Where sufficiently important, documents should not only be provided but signed copies obtained and filed.

Alternatively, documents may go up the line. For instance, you may consider that certain procedures require improvement; that machinery should be adapted or changed; or that more employees are needed for a particular operation, in the interests of safety. If you wish to be able to prove that you passed on this advice to higher authority, then put that advice into written form and keep a copy.

Warning the management

Are the company's top executives and managers aware of the legal risks to them personally? All are equally in peril. So everyone should be warned of his responsibility under the Act.

Conversely, has adequate training – including instructions and warnings arising from the Act – reached down to even the kitchen and canteen level? Do your procedures for establishing or maintaining communication between various levels of management on safety, health and welfare matters require overhaul?

Training

The Act specifically requires adequate training, in the interests of safety and health. Are your current training methods adequate at every level and are you giving sufficient authority to your training, personnel or safety officers or managers?

Consultations and committees

Responsibility on safety matters is spread over every level. Consultation should be aimed at ensuring that better and not worse relations are created due to the inevitable shared responsibility.

Regulations will inevitably be made, requiring consultation with workers through their 'recognized trade unions'. Have you established sufficient consultation, in advance? Safety committees will have to be set up in all businesses with recognized, independent trade unions. They should be created for the rest.

If you already operate a safety committee, are you satisfied that it meets sufficiently often; that there is sufficient involvement of both management and workers in its efforts; and that it has sufficient backing from the Board?

Supplying information

The Act recognizes that those fully informed on safety and health matters are least likely to suffer injury. Specific information is required under four heads. Are you ready to supply it?

- Employers are required by Section 2 to provide all necessary information to employees; this will be set out in the written statements and also in instructions concerning specific machinery or equipment.
- Section 2 requires occupiers to provide adequate information to visitors, contractors, neighbours and the general public. Take special care to ensure that visiting children and those who have charge of them (including cleaners and drivers) are fully and carefully warned of any special dangers to children in their care.
- Section 4 requires occupiers and those in control of non-domestic premises to provide adequate information to those who use equipment provided by them on such premises, which include not only self-service set-ups, launderettes and car parks, but also social and sporting clubs, provided or operated as part of the employer's undertaking.
- Section 6 requires many factories, designers, importers and suppliers (of plant, components and substances designed or intended for use at work) to provide all necessary information to users. The information should be supplied, wherever necessary, in writing. Is your documentation sufficient?

Problems for buyers

Section 6 (6) provides that there is no need to repeat testing or examination carried out by others; and where the buyer is supplied with a written undertaking by the seller, he is freed from his responsibility. Therefore, all buyers and purchasing departments should consider their procedures to ensure that they receive details of testing and examination carried out by their suppliers; and further to require the provision of written undertakings by all suppliers.

Conversely, sellers must be prepared to provide details of testing and of examination, plus written undertakings. Are these available for your customers?

59

Contributory Negligence

- As we have seen, you must look after your visitors, young and old, and take 'reasonable care' to keep your visitors safe.

- The younger the guest – wanted or unwanted – the greater the responsibility and the heavier the 'burden of care' which rests on you and your staff.

- So, what care are you entitled to expect your visitors to take for themselves?

Reasonable care

All visitors must take 'reasonable care' for their own safety. Your company or firm should carry ample insurance cover against liability towards your clients or customers. The premium, of course, will vary according to the risk and to your own safety record. But you are not the 'insurer' of your visitors. They are entitled to damages if, but only if, you have been negligent or in breach of some statutory duty. That, in its turn, depends not only on your safety standards but on the degree of care exercised by your guest, for his own protection.

Suppose that a father brings his little boy on to your premises. The child runs, trips and falls, fracturing his wrist. Are you liable? A court would ask the following questions. Did the accident happen entirely because you failed to take proper precautions for the safety of your child visitor? Were there enough staff, ensuring that youngsters did not run when it was dangerous to do so? Was the surface upon which the child slipped a dangerous one – perhaps because the flooring was worn or loose, defective or ancient? Alternatively, did the accident happen in spite of all due precautions on your part – perhaps because the father was not properly supervising his own child?

60

Your Liability for Your Employee's Negligence

- If your employee injures a fellow employee or a customer or a stranger while doing his job, can he be held liable at law – and can you?

- If, for instance, he causes an accident through his carelessness on the road, who is liable and can you dismiss the offender?

If an employee is negligent in the course of his employment, you are 'vicariously liable' to anyone who suffers injury, loss or damage as a result. Only if the employee was acting outside his employment – if he was on what lawyers charmingly call 'an independent frolic' – do you avoid liability.

Nor can you get an indemnity from your employee. The Court of Appeal ruled that if you were entitled to do so, then every employee would be claiming more money so that he could take out his own insurance.

Precisely the same rules apply on the road as they do in business. If your employee is negligent, you will be responsible. But if (for instance) the vehicle itself is defective then you as its owner are probably in breach of the Construction & Use Regulations.

Equally, if your employee creates a hazard either to other employees or to your customers because you have failed properly to train, instruct or supervise him, then you may be guilty of a criminal offence under the Health and Safety at Work Act. You must be prepared if necessary to prove that you have taken all such steps as are 'reasonably practicable' to protect both those whom you employ and others who are 'affected by your undertaking'.

Finally, if an employee is careless – whether in the business or on the road – and as a result the safety of other people is at risk, this may be a ground for dismissal. But all would depend upon the circumstances of the particular case, including whether or not the employee knew or ought to have known of the hazards and the fairness of your own procedures.

Section 7

Cases and Crimes

61

Courts and Claims

- **What are the civil and criminal courts?**
- **Can you get legal advice, and when?**
- **What are the latest rules on small claims?**

The civil law is designed to give individuals, companies and firms rights against each other. County Courts have jurisdiction (in general) for all claims up to £5,000. They also deal with small claims by special, swift and inexpensive procedures. Higher claims are brought in the High Court.

Criminal proceedings always start in Magistrates' Courts. If the accused is committed for trial 'on indictment' (by jury), then the case is heard in the Crown Court.

Appeals lie to the High Court, the Court of Appeal and (ultimately and rarely) to the House of Lords. Industrial tribunals, of course, deal (among others) with claims for unfair dismissal, redundancy and maternity rights. Appeals go to the Employment Appeal Tribunal, generally on points of law only – and thence to the Court of Appeal and to the House of Lords.

Legal aid rules are complicated and generally depend upon the nature of the case and on the 'disposable' income and capital of the applicant. It is not available to companies nor for industrial tribunal cases. But claimants in tribunals can get legal advice under the scheme which will help them to prepare for tribunal battle.

Scotland has equivalent courts, by other names. But the basic rules (like the vast bulk of employment law) are the same as in England and Wales.

62

How to Win Your Case

- If you have to go to court, how can you make the best of your chances?
- Here are some of the rules on winning.

If you are suing or sued in your individual capacity (or on behalf of a firm), then it is unwise to take a case as far as court without an experienced expert on your side.

If you operate through a company you are only entitled to appear in court through a lawyer. A company has no human existence – and even if its directors consider their lawyers as inhuman, they have the sole right of audience in court, on the corporation's behalf.

Choosing a lawyer

Horses for courses . . . and solicitors for cases. You have the choice. You could select a one-man band, whose sole attention you would get – but who may be harassed by other people's cases as well. Alternatively, you could select a small firm, with limited facilities – but still so interested in your problem that you will probably get a partner (or at least a senior legal executive) to look after you – and to deal with all your troubles.

Alternatively, you could choose a large firm – in which case, the chances are that each matter will be assigned to the partner or department which specializes in that type of legal trouble. You get the advantage of specialists – and the disadvantage that no one in the firm will know all your business.

Providing documents If your lawyer asks you for documents or statements, provide them. If you arrange appointments, keep them. The more co-operation you give your lawyers, the better results they will give you – and the lower your costs are likely to be.

Negligent solicitors If you have the misfortune to have negligent solicitors, then remember that they can be sued; if you can prove that you suffered damage (or, it appears, if you suffered mental anguish) because they were guilty of handling your affairs without due care, you will obtain damages from them. Or you could ask the Court to disallow the costs of your solicitor or to order him to pay the costs of your opponent.

Solicitors and barristers Solicitors deal with lay clients. They have a right of audience in lower courts or before tribunals. Barristers handle the worries of solicitors – and have a right to appear in any court in the land. They also give opinions and draft (or 'settle') pleadings (like Statements of Claim or Defence) and other complicated documents.

To win your case, you need the right barrister. But he will be chosen by your solicitor. You can express a preference, if you like – but just as a general practitioner in medicine will probably choose your surgeon or consultant, so it is generally best to let one lawyer choose the other.

Keep documents

Memories tend to fade and even honest witnesses may be in error. So contemporary documents are extremely important. An accurate filing system . . . letters which confirm contracts . . . even books which record the posting of mail – all these often win cases.

Wise businessmen either make or confirm important contracts in writing; send letters to dismissed employees, explaining their reasons; take care what they write. Even though an oral account is generally just as binding as a written one, it is far less easy to prove.

Witnesses

Try to have your witnesses available, ready and willing to appear. They can be dragged to court by the service of a subpoena (or forced to bring documents by a *subpoena doces tecum*) – but an unwilling witness tends to lose his memory.

If a witness finds it difficult to fit in the time to appear, the courts will usually do their best to meet his convenience. And if unfair questions are asked, the judge will normally intervene to protect a witness. Your object is to win your case – the object of the court is to ensure a fair trial – to see that justice is not only done, but (in the famous words of one judge) 'manifestly seen to be done'.

63

To Sue or Not to Sue

- **Litigation is a last resort.**
- **But how do you decide whether to write off a debt or whether to sue?**
- **Or whether, if you are sued, to pay up, seek a compromise or fight?**

The businessman should be spending his time making money, not in getting tied up with litigation. In fact, the great art of dealing with the law lies in keeping away from it. Litigation should be kept as a last resort only.

Still, when all else fails, you may be faced with the unhappy decision: to sue or not to sue. Take up the legal cudgels and you lose goodwill . . . risk getting a (probably entirely unjustified) reputation in the locality or in the trade for legal armtwisting . . . and you get embroiled in the (potentially very expensive) toils of the law. On the other hand, if all else fails, you either sue or wave farewell to your money.

A solicitor's letter

So consider: if you have taken all reasonable steps to get in your money and have failed – is it worth your while putting the matter in the hands of your solicitors – and when should you sue?

The first decision you have to take is commercial rather than legal. The businessman depends upon his personal good name and goodwill. Would legal action or even a solicitor's letter create more ill will than it is worth? Alternatively, is the debt so large that you cannot afford to lose it?

In many cases, a tactfully worded solicitor's letter does the trick. Your solicitor does not have to utter dire threats of legal action – at least not in the early stages. He could write something like this: 'Our clients, Messrs . . . have been most disturbed not to receive payment of their account for . . . , a copy of which we enclose herewith. They would be most reluctant to have to instruct us to take legal proceedings for the payment of this long outstanding debt. In the circumstances, we trust that we shall receive payment on our client's behalf, by return of post, so as to avoid the necessity for further action.'

There is a good chance that your clients or customers will pay your account, if they believe that you mean business. If they are reputable and potentially solvent, they will dislike the prospects of courting trouble, even more than you do. After all, their credit will dry up, if the world gets to know that they have to be sued for money they properly owe.

At best, the solicitor's initial 'letter before action' may get you in all the money you are owed. Alternatively, it may at least produce a reasonable offer of payment by instalments. At worst, it has cost you very little. To find out how much your solicitor would charge for opening up the battle – ask him. You will have to pay this charge, even if your customer then meets your account. You can only get legal costs from your debtors if you actually start your proceedings – or, possibly as part of an overall deal.

Proceeding to court

If the letter before action brings no results, then what? You must put a whole series of factors into the balance, before deciding whether or not to issue your writ or (usually in the case of a debt of £5,000 or less) your County Court summons.

- First, would it be worth your while to obtain a judgment? Suing a 'man of straw' is a fruitless pursuit.
- Again, if you were to press your claim, would the defendant find some defence which is at least arguable? Would he

194

contend, perhaps, that the machinery did not come up to expectations; that it broke down, that it was not in accordance with your promise?

- If there is a potentially valid defence, however tenuous, then you may be better off to come to some otherwise unreasonable compromise.

If there is no defence which is even arguable – in legal terms, no 'triable issue' – then your lawyers may manage to obtain 'summary' judgement. They can follow a procedure under Order 14 of the Rules of the Supreme Court which can enable a plaintiff to get his judgment without waiting for a case to get to trial. A similar procedure may now be used in a County Court. The jurisdiction of these lower Courts is now extended to debts up to £5,000 and application for summary judgment may be made if the case is begun by what is called a 'default summons', if the claim exceeds £500 and if the defendant files a defence. Naturally, if there is no defence filed, the plaintiff may apply for judgment in default of defence.

Legal costs   Finally, against the amount of the claim, you must set the potential amount of the legal costs. Remember that even if you win your case, the loser will probably only be forced to pay a proportion of your costs. The remainder will have to come out of your own pocket. Even if they were properly incurred, they may not be regarded by the Judge or Registrar who 'taxes' (or assesses) costs as having been so vital to your success that they should be laid at the loser's door.

'Taxing' costs

Costs may be 'taxed' or assessed on one of three bases:

- 'Party and party'.
- 'Common fund'.
- 'Solicitor and own client'.

'Party and party' is the normal basis and also least favourable to the winning party. All such costs as are 'necessary or proper for the attainment of justice or for enforcing or defending the rights of the party whose costs are being taxed' are normally permitted.

The 'common fund' basis applies where a party has conducted his case scandalously or fraudulently. This is more generous than a 'party and party' taxation but it will still not cover all costs incurred.

The 'solicitor and own client' basis applies as between each litigant and his own solicitor. In legal terms, this is the party's own personal liability to his solicitor.

Anyway, ask your solicitor to try to assess what the costs are likely to be. But do not expect a precise answer. So much will depend upon the nature and strength of the defences, the number of documents to be used or copied, the eminence and seniority of the lawyers 'briefed' on each side – and on many other factors.

So prepare the scales of justice. On one side put the size of the debt; the likelihood of getting your judgment and your money; matters of principle . . . and all those other factors in favour of suing. On the other scale put the costs of litigation; the ill will necessarily involved; the loss of your own time and that of your employee, in preparing for and engaging in the litigation; and the possibility that even if you get your judgment, the debtor may not be able to pay it.

The small businessman who wants to save on legal costs and go it alone, should first ensure that he is familiar with the provisions of the *Litigants in Person (Costs and Expenses) Act 1975*. He should be prepared to supply full details of time and expenses incurred in conducting his case. The Act allows the Courts to make orders for costs in favour of litigants in person.

When the costs are 'taxed', the Court can allow such costs as would have been allowed if the work had been done and disbursements paid out by a solicitor on a litigant's behalf. However in the case of what would have been a 'profit costs' item for a solicitor, the taxing officer cannot allow more than two-thirds of the sum which he would have allowed a solicitor. If the litigant has not actually suffered any pecuniary loss in doing the work, he cannot be allowed more than £2.00 per hour in respect of time reasonably spent by him on the work involved.

64

Time Limits

- **If you do not exercise your legal rights, you will lose them.**

- **So what are the 'periods of limitation' which the small businessman needs to know?**

In general, if you wish to sue someone, you have six years within which you must issue your High Court or your County Court summons. That 'period of limitation' generally begins when the right of action accrues.

Are you owed money? Then you do not have to start your legal proceedings until six years from the date when the debt actually fell due for payment. But once that date goes by, your right to claim it has vanished.

Accidents Or suppose that your vehicle is involved in a crash. You may sue for the cost of repairing the vehicle or hiring a replacement or for damage other than personal injuries at any time within six years from the accident.

Personal injury claims, though, must generally be brought within three years from the incident. But where a sufferer does not know of the injury, the legal clock starts ticking only when he does or should have that knowledge.

For instance, a man who worked in a noisy factory slowly became deaf. He could sue at any time within three years of the date when he should have realized that the work had caused his affliction.

These time limits have gradually been extended by courts, exercising their discretion. For instance, the foundations of a building cracked many years after it was completed. But only an extra cold winter followed by a blistering summer revealed the defect. It was held that those who had suffered were not disbarred until six years after the date when the defects became known.

An accountant was recently held liable to a client, many years after his negligent act. Clients have six years within which to sue from the time the negligence became known. .

Extensions of time

In the most recent case, the Appeal Court decided that courts have an absolute discretion to extend time periods in personal injury cases, where the interests of justice and of 'equity' so require.

Despite this trend, though, business people should take care to act swiftly and the basic principle remains – delay destroys rights. After all, time blurs memories, witnesses grow old and die and documents disappear. Or as one judge wittily put it: 'As time goes on, memory fades but recollection improves!'

Acting swiftly Even after issuing your proceedings, you must still act with reasonable despatch. If there has been 'unconscionable delay' your claim may be 'struck out for want of prosecution'. And while it is usually possible to prosecute people for crimes whenever the offences come to light and the offenders are found, cases must be pursued with reasonable speed.

First, there are some time limits which no court has the power to extend. For instance:

- 'Where reasonably practicable', an employee must bring his claim for unfair dismissal within three months from the date his employment terminates. Ignorance of the time limit is no excuse – and even if his delay is due to continuing negotiation or to long advice, his right dies along with the three months. Incidentally, in one case the Employment Appeal Tribunal decided that it is sufficient to push your application into the Tribunal's letter box before midnight on the last day of the three months. But the nature of the service which will be adequate in other cases varies – and it is not wise to wait until the last moment.

- As explained on page 49, if you are a business tenant and wish to retain your rights when your lease expires, then you must serve your counter-notice and, if necessary, apply to the court within specified times. No court has power to extend the limits, no matter how extenuating the circumstances.

How, then, are you most likely to pass your time limits? In business practice, wily debtors and potential defendants may 'without prejudice' admit liability and then drag out the negotiations until the time limit expires. Indeed, even if liability is admitted on the record, once the date of doom has passed, the rights have probably vanished.

The best way to avoid time risks? Let your lawyers get on with the job. If they let a due date pass so that you lose your rights, then they will most certainly have been negligent. Then whatever rights you would otherwise have had against the potential defendant will switch across to them. And because this is a reality, most solicitors are well insured against their own failings – and those of their staff.

In doubt? Anyway, if in doubt about time, at least start your proceedings. Keep the door open and your legal strength will remain. But once it slams closed, only the court's discretion may again allow you through – if you are lucky enough to come within the exceptions to the general rule that time limits are set to be observed.

65

Prosecution Law

- **What are the rules on prosecution for theft?**

- **Should you hand a suspect over to the police?**

- **In what circumstances will they prosecute?**

- **And if they suggest that you should prosecute, what should you consider before you sign the charge sheet?**

Checklist of main rules

- **It is pointless to prosecute if the accused is likely to be acquitted.**

So have you obtained a written confession? If so, did you remember to caution the suspect warning him that anything said would be taken down in writing and might be used in evidence? No caution would probably mean that no mention could be made of the confession in court.

- **Could you prove beyond all reasonable doubt that the culprit has acted dishonestly and that he intended 'permanently to deprive' you of the property taken?**

If he genuinely believed that he was entitled to the goods – perhaps as a 'perk' – or that if you had been asked for your permission to take them, you would have agreed, then prosecution would fail.

- **Assuming that you have a reasonable prospect of making the prosecution 'stick', but the accused is acquitted, could he show that you brought that prosecution out of 'malice'?**

If so, then he would have a good civil action for damages for 'malicious prosecution'. He would have to prove that you put him at risk out of a desire to harm him or for some other unlawful motive, and not because of your wish to see justice done. The mere fact that the prosecution fails will not of itself give any rights to the accused.

- **Is the accused a member of a minority group, extra sensitive to any unfairness?**

If so, then be especially careful and tactful.

- **Have you enough evidence – oral or documentary – to prove your case?**

If it is your word against that of the accused, and the burden of providing the case rests upon you, then you would probably be wise not to proceed.

- **Are you sure that you wish to prosecute?**

A civil action may be withdrawn at any time on payment of the costs of both sides. A criminal prosecution may only be withdrawn with leave of the court – which will only be given for an excellent reason and not (for instance) because you now feel sorry for the accused or because you realize that the prosecution will bring bad publicity on to your business.

- **Will a prosecution lead to trouble with others in your workforce?**

You must consider whether or not it is in the best interests of your business to prosecute – to discourage thefts by others or because you have a specific policy that all those caught thieving are handed over to the law. Will the prosecution add to the temptation for other employees by (for instance) revealing a shrewd mode of dishonesty which they have probably not thought of? Will a prosecution lead to bad publicity because it will show how poorly the person concerned was paid by comparison with his responsibilities; the extent of the temptation open to him; or the inadequate system which you have operated for the protection of your property?

- **Are there special mitigating circumstances in the case of the individual concerned which would encourage you not to prosecute?**

Consider the following:

1 Is the theft a minor one and the employee a person whom you wish to keep on your books, in spite of his slip from grace?

2 Is the employee a person who has given long service to you, to your company or firm; a man from a decent background; a family man with heavy responsibilities; a normally decent person who acted in an uncharacteristic way under particular stress – ill-health or debt?

3 Is the employee willing to resign – or will you wish to dismiss him – and do you feel that the loss of his job is sufficient punishment, both from his point of view and from that of others who will hear of your decision?

- **What are the views of the police as to the prosecution?**

How far are they prepared to help? Do they consider that the prosecution is likely to succeed? And what is their estimate of the length of the trial?

- **If you are asked to prosecute, what are the costs likely to be?**

Assuming that the prosecution is brought properly, your legal expenses may be recoverable from the Central Fund, even if the prosecution fails. Consult your solicitor to find out what risk there may be to your pocket.

- **How much time would have to be devoted by how many (and which) of your staff, if the appropriate evidence is to be placed before the court?**

If the accused pleads guilty, both the costs and the time will be reduced; but a plea of not guilty will inevitably involve time – and possibly anxiety.

- **Finally, if the offender is convicted, is he likely to receive such leniency that other potential offenders will actually be encouraged?**

If the case is likely to be heard by your local bench, how do they generally treat pilferers, petty thieves or other villains of the category concerned?

Having checked the list, if you are still in doubt then consult your solicitor. If you prosecute privately, you will in any event need help. So get it before you make your decision, if you are in any doubt what the decision should be.

66

Burden of Proof

- **If you are prosecuted for a business offence, is it inevitable that the prosecution will have to prove its case against you 'beyond all reasonable doubt'?**

The general rule is that the jury must be 'satisfied so that they feel sure' of the guilt of the accused. But there are exceptions. The most important are:

- If you are prosecuted under the Health and Safety at Work Act and (as is likely) your defence is: 'We did all that was reasonably practicable to avoid creating or perpetuating the hazard', then you will have to prove your innocence. 'It shall be for the accused to show', says the Act, that the hazard proved was not his fault – or alternatively, that it was 'due to the act or default of some other person'.

- If you are charged with bribing an employee of local or national government or of a nationalized industry, then once it has been shown that you gave or attempted to give – or that the other party received or attempted to get – an inducement, then the dishonest and corrupt motive is presumed. It will be for you to prove, if you can, that you acted with propriety.

- Under the Food and Drugs Acts, if a foreign body is present in food, then those who served it are presumed to have been guilty of an offence under that Act.

These of course are rare exceptions to the general rule that it is for the prosecution to satisfy the court of the guilt of the accused. And while the standard of proof in a civil action is 'the balance of probabilities', in a criminal case, proof must be 'beyond all reasonable doubt'.

67

Theft

- **Small businesses are as likely to be prey to thieves as larger ones.**

- **So what should you *know* about the law on theft?**

The offence of 'larceny' has been abolished. In its place: 'A person is guilty of theft if he dishonestly appropriates property belonging to another with the intention of permanently depriving the other of it.' Whether the taking is made 'with a view to gain' – so that the goods may be sold – or 'for a thief's own benefit' is irrelevant. Call it 'shoplifting', 'fiddling', 'shrinkage', or whatever name is appropriate – in law it is 'theft'.

'Perks'

An appropriation is not regarded as dishonest if done 'in the belief that the taker has in law the right to deprive the other of it'. So taking the off-cuts from the factory floor – or anything else – in the honest (but misguided) belief that these are part of the 'perks' of the employment, is not theft.

Again, 'If he appropriates the property in the belief that he would have the owner's consent, if the owner knew of the appropriation and the circumstances of it' the taker has a good defence. Finally, 'If he appropriates the property in the belief that the person to whom the property belongs cannot be discovered by taking reasonable steps', he will not be guilty of theft. The converse still applies. Find goods and fail to take reasonable steps to trace the owner, but merely dispose of them or use them for your own purpose, and you are guilty of theft.

Borrowing

In general, borrowing is still no crime. But a borrowing is illegal if the taker's 'intention is to treat the thing as his own to dispose of regardless of the owner's rights'.

Receiving

First, know from whom you buy. Even if goods turn out to be stolen, if you can identify the seller and show that you have cause to trust him, you will be let off the legal hook. What then happens to him is his concern.

Next, look at the circumstances of the sale and see whether they are even apparently honest. If a fellow appears in the dead of night, for instance, send him on his way.

Then do make sure you obtain a full receipt, setting out the name and address of the seller; identifying him, if possible (perhaps by the number of his car, van or driving licence); describing the goods; bearing the seller's signature – and also saying that the goods belong to the seller and (in appropriate cases) are not the subject of any charge or outstanding hire purchase agreement.

Recording purchases   Naturally, all purchases should go through the books. But even if some escape the formal, accounting net, you must make absolutely certain that any casual purchase, the origin – and basis of which is potentially in doubt, is entered into your ledgers – and can be traced going out of them. The greater the bargain . . . the less you know the seller . . . the more suspicious the deal could look, to the trained police mind . . . the more vital it is that you can show that you dealt with the matter in an entirely normal way.

In fact, the police should be consulted before you buy, if there is ever any real doubt. Say to the seller: 'Look, I don't know you. I have an arrangement with the local police that when I buy in this way, I have them check their books on the goods beforehand. Have you any objection?' If there is the least flinching on the part of the seller, do not buy. If he agrees, then you may still check with the authorities. By the time you come back from the telephone, the dishonest man will probably have disappeared.

Above all, remember that if the circumstances are sufficiently suspicious, a jury might well take the view that you must have known that the goods were 'hot' . . . that you were dishonest . . . that you either 'knew' or 'believed' that they were stolen. It is sometimes very difficult to believe that the honest businessman who falls for a dishonest bargain is as simple as he would like to seem. And when it comes to buying, it is up to you to see that you do not buy stolen goods. If in doubt, say no.

Naturally, it is up to the prosecution to prove beyond reasonable doubt that the accused 'handler' knew or believed that the goods concerned were stolen. A dishonest intent is not presumed against the purchaser. But where a purchase is made in suspicious circumstances; where the price is low and the buyer has taken insufficient precautions; where the books are inadequate and the buyer's excuses likewise – then it may take good fortune to be acquitted. To be tried and found innocent is excellent; it is much better never to be tried at all.

So when you are offered a bargain by a stranger, take care. You may find it much more expensive than it seems.

68

Bribery-and Business Gifts

- **When is it lawful to make or to take a business gift?**
- **Is there a difference at Christmas time?**
- **When is goodwill 'corrupt'?**

Corruption

The difference between a genuine, lawful gift and the giving of a criminal bribe lies in one word: 'corruption'. If the gift is open and above board, then it is lawful; if it is underhand – whether by way of so called 'commission', 'payola' or 'greasing the palm', 'slush', 'dash', 'the drop', 'dropsy', 'backhanders' or any other form of bribery – then it is unlawful.

The Prevention of Corruption Acts make it a serious offence to offer or to give money or anything else as an 'inducement' to the getting of a very good 'favour' in return. And the person who bribes or who attempts to obtain a bribe is just as guilty of the same offence (and liable to exactly the same penalties) as the man who attempts to benefit from the corrupt practice.

For the ordinary businessman, there is a presumption of innocence. Whether you give or whether you receive a Christmas kindness, it will be presumed in your favour that no corruption was intended. The prosecution must prove not only the act but also its corrupt intent.

'Public servants'

The public servant, on the other hand, is in a dangerous and vulnerable position. If it is proved that he received a gift, then it will be presumed that it was both given and received 'corruptly'. So employees of Government, local authorities or other public bodies are generally very careful indeed not to receive presents – even at Christmas time. And if you deal with any department of any authority (local or national) – take care. Do not put yourself or your contacts in peril from the law. When dealing with private individuals, the law provides a maximum sentence of two years' imprisonment and an unlimited fine – but an employee of a public body may be sent to jail for up to seven years, and fined in addition such sum as the court thinks fit.

Give openly

So how do you give a 'gift or money or other consideration or reward', in the hope that the recipient will 'show favour or disfavour', without risking trouble?

The more openly you endeavour to behave, the less likely you are to run into trouble. Send your gift to the man's home and immediately there is an implication that you are doing so furtively and in the hope that his bosses will not know. Send it to the office or works and you are showing not only goodwill but also bona fides – good faith.

Suppose that you employ a manager and give him considerable power to buy on your behalf. Suppose that he gets a bottle or a crate of whisky at Christmas time, and it arrives at your premises. He says to you: 'May I keep it?' You then have the alternatives. You can agree; or you can say: 'We'll have it for our Christmas party' – or you may tell him to send it back.

Now suppose that the gift arrives at your employee's home. You find out about it afterwards – and may be justifiably furious. You will want your manager to buy without feeling that he must favour his benefactor.

Bribery

Then take one step further. Suppose (as, unfortunately, often happens in both commerce and industry) an important buyer is given a secret commission. This may be in the form of cash or of some 'benefit in kind'. This comes to him tax-free and may be a very important addition to his income. If he accepts it, then he is acting 'corruptly' and is liable, if caught, to be imprisoned. Naturally, his employer may sack him. He may also be required to disgorge his ill-gotten gains.

Meanwhile, the bribed man is in a dangerous position. He may be blackmailed; he cannot very well complain about the quality or quantity of the goods delivered – and the supplier can put up his price to meet the extra 'commission' without fear of complaint from the man whom he has placed in his pay.

The larger the outfit, the more likely it is that you will have to deal with these problems. But even if you run a modest enterprise, you should be aware of their existence. And when the Christmas season approaches, you should mind how, what and to whom you give – and should consider a little before you accept a gift – particularly one that is particularly munificent and is obviously given with the hope of obtaining some future favour.

Finally, what of the case where the person bribed (to use the words of the Lord Chief Justice) 'double crossed, and did not do what he was bribed for'. That, said the judge, ' is no reason why he should be acquitted of taking a bribe'.

So it is no defence to say: 'I did not do as I was asked' – nor 'He double-crossed me'. Briber and bribed; offeror and offeree; the one with the cash or the benefit in kind and the one who wants it – both are equally guilty. And secret bribes or commission are 'corrupt' – even when disguised as 'Christmas gifts'. And even if the 'generosity' does not produce the results hoped for, both briber and bribed may spend their Christmas behind the wrong kind of bars.

69

Finding

- **Who owns lost property?**

'Finders, keepers', is, was and will be a thoroughly misleading old maxim. The basic law – which remains unchanged even after the *Theft Act 1968* came into force – is that, unless actually and deliberately abandoned, lost goods belong to their true owner.

Suppose, then, that you find goods which have been left on your premises – whether by a client or customer, supplier's representative, previous occupier or person unknown. You do not acquire ownership of the goods, simply because you find them. Only if the true owner does not turn up will the finder normally have the next best claim. Even here there are three exceptions. If the finding is done by an employee in the course of his employment, his findings (like his work – and his mistakes) will be on behalf of the boss. Then the chain runs: true owner, employer, finder.

If the goods found are gold, silver or bullion deliberately hidden, then they are 'treasure trove' and belong to the Crown. If the find is reported, the finder should get compensation.

A person is not guilty of theft 'if he appropriates . . . property in the belief that the person to whom the property belongs cannot be discovered by taking reasonable steps'. Except where the property comes to him as trustee or personal representative, then, the finder of property is entitled to appropriate it provided that he believes that the true owner 'cannot be discovered by taking reasonable steps'. But if he simply pockets the money . . . sells the goods . . . or otherwise 'appropriates' the items found, without taking reasonable steps to trace their owner, he is guilty of theft – and liable to be imprisoned for up to ten years for his (lack of) trouble.

So if you or your staff find goods, do take every reasonable step to trace the owner. If you want to be quite sure that no dishonest intent can be imputed to you, inform the police before you dispose of the goods for your own benefit. But keep the goods found without trying to trace the owner and you may be gaoled for theft.

In Conclusion

The object of the law? To provide a sensible structure, to regulate a decent and intelligent society. The civil law gives rights to citizens – individually or as organized in (for instance) companies, partnerships or trade unions. The criminal law imposes minimum standards on behalf of society as a whole.

Anyway, the law is there to help and to guide. With this book at your side for reading and for reference, I hope that your contacts with the law will be constructive, painless and as inexpensive as possible.

Remember: the rules in this book are intended as a guide to the small businessman and not as a substitute for legal help on specific issues. Still, follow the rules and you should need help less often and it should prove far more effective.

Useful Addresses

Advisory, Conciliation and Arbitration Service (ACAS)
11–12 St James Square, London SW1
(01-214 6000)

Advertising Standards Authority
Brook House, 2–16 Torrington Place, London WC1E 7HN
(01-580 5555)

Association of British Chambers of Commerce
Sovereign House, 212a Shaftesbury Avenue, London WC2
(01-240 5831)

Association of British Travel Agents
55–57 Newman Street, London W1P 4AH
(01-637 2444)

Association of Independent Businesses
Torowbray House, 108 Weston Street, London SE1 3QB
(01-403 4066)

British Council
10 Spring Gardens, London SW1A 2BN
(01-930 8466)

British Institute of Management (Management Information Unit)
Management House, Parker Street, London WC2B 5PT
(01-405 3456)

British Library
2 Sheraton Street, London W1V 4BH
(01-636 1544)

British Overseas Trade Board
1 Victoria Street, London SW1H 0ET
(01-215 7877)

British Standards Institution
2 Park Street, London W1A 2BS
(01-629 9000)

British Telecommunications
2–12 Gresham Street, London EC2V 7AG
(01-432 1234)

British Tourist Authority (Head Office)
Queen's House, 64 St James's Street, London SW1A 1NF
(01-629 9191)

Business Books Ltd
17–21 Conway Street, London W1P 6JD
(01-387 2811)

Central Office of Information
Hercules Road, London SE1 7DU
(01-928 2345)

Charity Commission
14 Ryder Street, St James's, London SW1Y 6AH
(01-214 6000)

Citizens Advice Bureau (London Enquiries)
31 Wellington Street, London WC2
(01-379 6841)

Commission for Racial Equality
Elliot House, 10–12 Allington Street, London SW1B 5EH
(01-828 7022)

Companies' Registration Office
Companies House, Crown Way, Maindy, Cardiff CF4 3UZ
(0222 388588)

Company Registration Office (London Search Room)
55–71 City Road, London EC1Y 1BB
(01-253 9393)

Confederation of British Industry
103 New Oxford Street, London WC1A 1DU
(01-379 7400)

Conservative Central Office
32 Smith Square, London SW1
(01-222 9000)

Council of Small Industries in Rural Areas (COSIRA)
141 Castle Street, Salisbury SP1 3TP, Wiltshire
(0722 6255)

Customs and Excise
King's Beam House, Mark Lane, London EC3R 7HE
(01-626 1515)

Design Council
28 Haymarket, London SW1 4SU
(01-839 8000)

Director of Public Prosecutions
4–12 Queen Anne's Gate, London SW1
(01-213 3000)

EEC Information Unit
Department of Industry, Millbank Tower, Millbank, London SW1P 4QX
(01-211 7060)

Electricity Council
30 Millbank, London SW1P 4RD
(01-834 2333)

Employment, Department of
Caxton House, Tothill Street, London SW1H 9NA
(01-213 3000)

Equal Opportunities Commission
Overseas House, Quay Street, Manchester M3 3HN
(061-833 9244)

European Parliament (United Kingdom Office)
2 Queen Anne's Gate, London SW1H 9AA
(01-222 0411)

Export Credits Guarantee Department
Aldermanbury House, Aldermanbury Square, London EC2P 2EL
(01-606 6699)
or Crown Building, Cathay's Park, Cardiff CF1 3NH
(0222 31033)

Gaming Board for Great Britain
Berkshire House, 168–173 High Holborn, London WC1V 7AA
(01-240 0821)

Government Hospitality Fund
2 Carlton Gardens, London SW1Y 5AA
(01-214 6000)

Health and Safety Commission
Regina House, 259–269 Old Marylebone Road, London NW1 5RR
(01-723 1262)

Health and Safety Executive
Baynard House, 1 Chepstow Place, London W2
(01-229 3456)

Health and Social Security, Department of
Alexander Fleming House, Elephant and Castle, London SE1 6BY
(01-407 5522)

Her Majesty's Stationery Office (HMSO)
Sovereign House, Botolph Street, Norwich NR3 1DN
(0603 22211)

Home Office
50 Queen Anne's Gate, London SW1H 9AT
(01-213 5100)

House of Commons
London SW1A 0AA
(01-219 3000)

Industrial Relations Services Training
67 Maygrove Road, London NW6 2EJ
(01-328 4751)

Industrial Tribunals Central Office (England and Wales)
93 Ebury Bridge Road, London SW1W 8RE
(01-730 9161-7)

Industrial Injuries Advisory Council
Friars House, 157–168 Blackfriars Road, London SE1 8EU

Industry, Department of
123 Victoria Street, London SW1E 6RB
(01-212 7676)
(*see also* Small Firms Service)

Inland Revenue
Somerset House, Strand, London WC2R 1LB
(01-438 6622)

Labour Party
150 Walworth Road, London SE17 1JT
(01-703 0833)

Land Registry
Lincoln's Inn Fields, London WC2A 3PH
(01-405 3488)

Law Society
113 Chancery Lane, London WC2
(01-242 1222)

Legal Aid Regional Offices

London South Area Law Society (No. 1 Legal Aid Area)
29–37 Red Lion Street, London WC1R 4PP
(01-405 6991)

South Eastern Area Law Society (No. 2 Legal Aid Area)
9–12 Middle Street, Brighton BN1 1AS
(0273 27003)

Southern Area Law Society (No. 3 Legal Aid Area)
Crown House, 10 Crown Street, Reading RG1 2SJ
(0734 589696)

South Western Area Law Society (No. 4 Legal Aid Area)
Whitefriars Block C, Lewins Mead, Bristol BS1 2LR
(0272 214801)

South Wales Area Law Society (No. 5 Legal Aid Area)
Third Floor, Marland House, Central Square, Cardiff CF1 1PF
(0222 388971)

West Midland Area Law Society (No. 6 Legal Aid Area)
Polium Centre, City House, 5 Hill Street, Birmingham B5 4UD
(021-632 6541)

North Western Area Law Society (No. 7 Legal Aid Area)
67 King's Street, Manchester M60 9AX
(061-832 7112)

North East Area Law Society (No. 8 Legal Aid Area)
18 Newgate Shopping Centre, Newcastle-upon-Tyne NE1 5RU
(0632 23461)

North Eastern Area Law Society (No. 9 Legal Aid Area)
City House, New Station Street, Leeds LS1 4JS
(0532 442851)

East Midlands Area Law Society (No. 10 Legal Aid Area)
5 Friar Lane, Nottingham NG1 6BW
(0602 412424)

Eastern Area Law Society (No. 11 Legal Aid Area)
Kett House, Station Road, Cambridge CB1 2JT
(0223 66511)

Chester and North Wales Area Law Society (No. 12 legal Aid Area)
Pepper House, Pepper Row, Chester CH1 1DW
(0244 315455)

London East Area Law Society (No. 13 Legal Aid Area)
29–37 Red Lion Street, London WC1R 4PP
(01-405 6991)

London West Area Law Society (No. 14 Legal Aid Area)
29–37 Red Lion Street, London WC1R 4PP
(01-405 6991)

Merseyside Area Law Society (No. 15 Legal Aid Area)
Moore House, James Street, Liverpool L2 7SA
(051-236 8371)

Liberal Party
1 Whitehall Place, London SW1
(01-839 4092)

Manpower Services Commission
Selkirk House, 166 High Holborn, London WC1V 6PB
(01-836 1213)

Monopolies and Mergers Commission
New Court, 48 Carey Street, London WC2A 2JE
(01-831 6111)

National Consumer Council
18 Queen Anne's Gate, London SW1H 9AA
(01-222 9501)

National Economic Development Council (NEDC)
Millbank Tower, Millbank, London SW1P 4QX
(01-211 3000)

National Federation of Self-employed and Small Businesses Ltd
32 St Anne's Road West, Lytham St Annes, Lancashire FY8 1NY
(0253 720911)

Office of Fair Trading
Field House, 15–25 Breams Building, London EC4A 1PR
(01-242 2858)

Passport Office
Clive House, 70–78 Petty France, London SW1H 9HD
(01-213 3000)

Patent Office
25 Southampton Buildings, Chancery Lane, London WC2A 1AY
(01-405 8721)

Science and Engineering Research Council
Polaris House, North Star Avenue, Swindon, Wiltshire SN2 1ET
(0793 26222)

Scottish Consumer Council
4 Somerset Place, Glasgow G3 7JT
(041-332 8858)

Scottish Development Agency
120 Bothwell Street, Glasgow G2 7JP
(041-248 2700)
London Office: 17 Cockspur Street, London SW1Y 5BL
(01-839 2117)

Scottish Development Department
New St Andrew's House, St James Centre, Edinburgh EH1 3PB
(031-556 8400)

Scottish Office
Dover House, Whitehall, London SW1A 2AU
(01-233 3000)

Small Firms Service The Department of Industry administers the Small Firms Service through regional centres. They provide small businesses with a free information service covering a wide range of subjects from sources of supply to government legislation. Regional centres may be contacted by dialling 100 and asking the operator for Freephone 2444. The following are the addresses of the main regional offices:

Head Office, Small Firms Division, DOI
Ashdown House, 123 Victoria Street, London SE1E 6RB
(01-212 0629)

Northern Region
R22, Centro House, 3 Cloth Market, Newcastle-upon-Tyne NE1 3EE
(0632 32535)

North West Region
3rd Floor, 320–325 Royal Exchange Buildings, St Anne's Square, Manchester M2 7AH
(061-832 5282)

Yorkshire and Humberside
1 Park Row, City Square, Leeds LS1 5NR
(0532 445151)

West Midlands Region
6th Floor, Ladywood House, Stephenson Street, Birmingham B2 4DT
(021-643 3344)

East Midlands Region
Severns House, 20 Middle Pavement, Nottingham NG1 7DW
(0602 581205)

Eastern Region
24 Brooklands Avenue, Cambridge CB2 2BU
(0223 63312)

South Western Region
5th Floor, The Pithay, Bristol BS1 2NB
(0272 294546)

South Eastern Region
Ebury Bridge House, 2–18 Ebury Bridge Road, London SW1 8QD
(01-730 8451)

Scotland
120 Bothwell Street, Glasgow G2 7TU
(041-248 6014)

Wales
16 St David's House, Wood Street, Cardiff CF1 1ER
(0222 396116)

Small Firms Technical Enquiry Service (SFTES)
Melton Mowbray, Leicestershire LE13 0PB
(0664 64133)

Social Democratic Party
4 Cowley Street, London SW1
(01-222 4141)

Trade, Department of
1 Victoria Street, London SW1 0ET
(01-215 7877)

Transport, Department of
2 Marsham Street, London SW1P 3EB
(01-212 3434)

Travel Association Consultative Council
55–57 Newman Street, London W1P 4AH
(01-637 2444)

Value Added Tax Tribunal
17 North Audley Street, London W1Y 2PX
(01-629 5544)

Welsh Consumer Council
Oxford House, Hills Street, Cardiff CF1 2DR
(0222 396056)

Welsh Office

London Office: Gwydyr House, Whitehall, London SW1A 2ER
(01-233 3000)
Cardiff Office: Crown Buildings, Cathays Park, Cardiff CF1 3NQ
(0222 825111)

Index

225

title in, 117; less than three months, for, 131; medical examination under, 118; mobility clauses in, 117; moonlighting and, 117–18; notices under, *see* notice *under* employee; procedures set out in, 118–19; restraint clauses in, 115–16, 118; sick pay under, 130; signatures to, 119; temporary employee and, 167–8; terms of, 26–7, 117–19, 168, 178–9
enforcement notice, 59–60
evidence, 202
expenses, 28, 36–7
export, 84

factory inspector, 177, 180
finding, 212–13
fire, 179
Food and Drugs Acts, 205
foreigners, 125
fraud, 23, 92, 101

grievance procedure, 167
guarantee: assignment of lease, upon, 106; cheque, of, 98; contract of, 72; contractual rules and, 86; sale, upon, 67–8
guarantee cards, 98

health and safety: Acts covering, 173; administration of Act, 175; charging employees not allowed, 175; claim for damages, 176; code, 177, 179–80; consultation about, 181; contract of employment and, 178; defective products, 85, 87–8; documentation, 180–2; employee protection, 27, 127 176, 182; information, 182; insurance, 180, 184; liability, 27, 174–7, 181–5; penalties under the Act, 175; procedure, 179, 182–3; prosecution under the Act, 204; public protection, 177, 182, 184; Regulations, 155, 175, 177; responsibility of employee, 176, 178, 181; rules, 173; safety clothing, 175, 179; safety committee, 181–2; safety representatives, 155, 178; temporary employee, 168; training, 181; written policy, 174, 180, 182; *see*

also medical examination
hire purchase, 72, 79
holidays, 120
home, 37–8, 57
hours of work, 153–5, 164, *see also* overtime *and* short-time

import, 84
incapacity for work, 131
industrial tribunal: action for discrimination, 123; award of costs by, 159–60; closing down business, upon, 108; constructive dismissal and, 142–3; disputes and, 168; legal advice before, 189; maternity rights and, 189; 'pre-hearing assessment' by, 159–60; redundancy and, 142, 189; trade unions and, 108; unfair dismissal and, 26, 123, 141–3, 189
injunction, 115
injury, 198–9
insolvency, 101–4, 137
insurance: broken, 90; claims, 90–2; company, 92; contract, 72; employer's liability, 27; goods in transit, of, 74; health and safety, 180; liability towards customers, 184; material facts affecting, 90–2; overvaluation, 91; policy, 89–91; product liability, 87; proposal, 90; purchase of, 89–90, 92; terms of, 89
interest, 96–7
inventions, 118

job title, 117

land sale, 72
larceny, 206
leave, *see* holidays *and* sick pay
legal aid, 185
liability: contractual, 85; customers, towards, 184; employers', 176–7; Health and Safety Act, under, 27, 174–7, 181–5; limited, 19, 28; occupier's, 177; partnership, 20–1, 28; product, 85–8; strict, 87
liquidator, 103
litigation, 150, 193, 196–7
loan, 95–6

227

Starting the business. Here's how to keep it

The key to keeping your business going is to keep it growing. That means you need more people to help you, bigger premises, more customers and maybe even new products. And as your company grows, your accounts get more complex and less understandable. Suddenly your small business isn't so small any more, and it's hard to keep control.

The only way to cope is to call in the experts. The new *Building Your Business* series is a unique collection of tips and techniques from top business consultants who have already experienced *and solved* the problems you're facing now. Each book is packed with practical business know-how to help *you* keep *your* business going and growing.

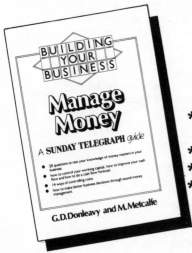

* how to answer your bank manager's questions
* 14 ways to control your costs
* how to do a cash flow forecast
* how good money management helps you make better business decisions

* how to keep your customers satisfied
* all you need to know about market research, pricing, advertising, developing new products and exporting
* how to sell the *sizzle* not the sausage
* the information you need, and how to use it

was your first problem.
going and growing.

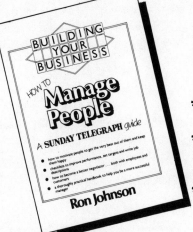

*   how to get the best out of people *and*
    keep them happy
*   checklists for improving performance,
    setting targets and writing job
    descriptions
*   how to be a better negotiator — both
    with your employees and your customers

Building Your Business books are
available from your local bookseller.
You can also order copies direct from
Business Books, using the form
below.